Published by Dove

M000251975

ISBN# 0-9668528-3-4

Second Printing, 2005

This work is dedicated to David Michael Newman, who is loved by his parents, grandparents, godparents, and the enormous group of our family and friends we are lucky enough to have surrounding him.

Cover Design

Our deep thanks to Ken Braun, founder and CEO of Lounge Lizard Worldwide, for our book cover concept. Thanks also to Lounge Lizard's creative director, Greg Kubacki, for bringing Ken's vision to life. See more examples of their great work at www.loungelizard.com

Table of Contents

Foreword by Frederica Blausten, p. v

Section One: Why a Graduated ABA Model?

Section Two: Basic ABA Ideas, to be Adapted to Guide Thinking at Each Level of Programming

Section Three: A Longitudinal Study

Appendices: Some Summary Presentations

References and Suggested Readings, p. 142

Foreword

There are many laboratory schools in existence, where the findings of behavioral science are implemented to address behavioral and educational issues. These programs tend to be small and are few and far between, however, and they cannot serve the vast numbers that require their services. They often also make minimal impact beyond the families and children they directly serve. This book demonstrates that it is possible to synthesize theory and practice into a single model within a large agency.

General education suffers over what constitutes the most effective practice. Evaluators run experimental programs or replication sites, but rarely do these innovations spread into long-term practice or more generalized use. Special education suffers even more, as there are so many different ideas regarding what constitutes progress. There are also a multitude of ways to explain lack of progress; blame the staff, blame the disability, blame the child, blame the parents, etc. The relative newness of special education for autistic children introduces unique difficulties, as there is not even extensive history to fall back upon.

This book demonstrates that it is possible to synthesize theory and solid research to produce a relatively large organization that puts into practice the best of applied behavioral science. Dr. Newman has drawn on his depth of professional expertise in the field of Applied Behavior Analysis (ABA) to help AMAC to realize its vision. In fact, he is jokingly referred to as the "Dark Overlord of ABA," as his role at AMAC for the past six years has been to be our "overseer," to ensure AMAC's adherence to data-based best practice. Some schools dabble in the use of behavioral principles, particularly when politics make such practices "hot." Then there's AMAC, which is not just a model, not just a pilot, but a long-term operating program whose systems are not an experiment, but are in everyday use with hundreds of children.

AMAC is successful because it is a monothetic model. This philosophy dictates the use of a single methodology, which a public school system can not and does not do. Unfortunately, because of the vagueness of IDEA, methodology is not able to be mandated in Individualized Education Plans. This failure to mandate data-based methodologies leads to blind alleys. First we had a "blame the parents" model. Then we had a "blame the child" model, followed by "blame the medication," (if not Haldol, then what?). Now we're up to the "blame the treatment" model, which is where it belongs. If a treatment doesn't stand up to scientific scrutiny, whether this treatment features drugs, diets, dolphins, auditory or sensory integration training, or deep pressure, then it should not be implemented. The educated consumer, be it a parent or professional, must always make well-informed, data-based decisions. When doctors study medication and make those decisions, it is honest and fair and based on solid data. It is regrettable that in education, research-based scientific decision-making is not required when choosing a methodology or a course of treatment. AMAC demonstrates that the scientific choice continues to be the right choice. AMAC is not an experiment. It is an on-going organization that remains healthy because data-based treatment methodologies based on solid learning theory are in place. At the root, there is a commitment from the Board of Directors, Executive Director, and families and the staff to this data-based stance, and all are accountable to that commitment.

We need to acknowledge the models and the pilots, beginning in the 1970's and 1980's, which laid the groundwork for AMAC. These include: Dr. Ogden Lindsley, "Precision Teaching" in Kansas, Dr. Ray Romanczyk at SUNY Binghamton (whose application of technology to curriculum and data collection well preceded anyone's use of personal computers for organizational management and quality control), Dr. Ira Cohen for his "wheel" that addressed scheduling plans for reinforcement and for his neuronet studies that led to new models of programming, Dr. Matthew Israel's super multimedia reward store designs/implementations, Dr. Richard Foxx's positive reinforcement practices, and our own Dr. Bobby Newman's self-help programs and parent and staff training systems. Lastly, let us acknowledge those New York State government officials (Larry Gloeckler and Tom Hamel), who recognized that scientific methodology and best practice can be delivered cost-effectively only when officials are collaborative and committed to children.

This book is the mirror of the graduated applied behavioral model. Dr. Newman reminds us that when theory and practice are one, results are outstanding; just keep at it. Thank you, Bobby, for the reflection.

Frederica Blausten, M.A., M.S.
Executive Director,
AMAC, March, 2002

Section One: Why a Graduated ABA Model?

Chapter One: Graduated ABA

This manual will describe the system that I like to call Graduated Applied Behavior Analysis (GABA) ™. In actuality, however, I believe that it is basically just good "old fashioned" Applied Behavior Analysis (ABA) and nothing special. In truth, I was hesitant to put a name on it. This is nothing more or less than what the wonderful people who introduced me to ABA taught about how to consider our discipline and how to carry out its techniques. Do not, under penalty of death by having to read the sections on whale anatomy in *Moby Dick*, call it "doing Newman" or any other such name. I myself argued that associating surnames with techniques or approaches was downright silly (Newman, in press). I'm only putting a name on it so that there is something to call it to distinguish it from other systems within ABA (e.g., CABAS™, Verbal Behavior, Pivotal Response Training, etc.). I will argue that each of these systems is actually located well within ABA, and differ only in teaching priorities, prompting strategies, and behavioral measures.

This should never have become something akin to religious factions arguing over which is the true gospel (nor will I quote Jesus' statement about not coming to destroy the law, but to fulfill it). As I will hammer home again and again, ABA is a data-based discipline. As long as one is thinking and acting in a data-based fashion as guided by solid learning theory and following the ethical guidelines accepted by the professional ethics boards, one is doing good ABA. I call this particular presentation "Graduated" only in an effort to address the statements outlined in the paragraph that follows.

This manual is being written in response to three main statements that I have been hearing increasingly often within the last five years:

1.   *I was told that my child is too high-functioning for ABA.*

2.   *My consultant, Dr. Gimmeitsmine, has described how outdated and oppressive ABA is, and showed how his system is much better for making the child happy and teaching skills.*

3.   *We do a "modified ABA."*

Let's handle each of these, in turn. We'll begin with "I was told that my child is too high-functioning for ABA." This comment shows what has unfortunately happened to ABA in recent years. What people often actually mean when they say this is that they think their child is too high-functioning to require Discrete Trial Teaching (DTT). Unfortunately, of late Discrete Trial Teaching has become the tail that wags the dog in ABA. Lay people often fail to realize that Discrete Trial Teaching is just one of ABA's techniques. When these people say Applied Behavior Analysis, what they actually mean is DTT. You frequently hear the question phrased, "how many hours of ABA is he getting?" To use one of my lines that trainees are probably sick of: *"How many hours of ABA is a nonsensical question. Applied Behavior Analysis is not a related service. It is a 24 hour a day educational philosophy."*

Something I like to describe in training is the "culture" of ABA. When a program is being created, everyone must commit to ABA thinking and procedures. A common language and way of thinking and acting thus evolves, and this keeps everything consistent, 24 hours a day. Whenever students are not engaged in intensive teaching, their skills should still be practiced in generalized settings and behavior management strategies pursued every bit as intensively as during 1 to 1 teaching.

The need for carry-through outside of program time cannot be over-emphasized. This can quite literally mean the difference between a successful program that leads to generalized skills, and an unsuccessful program where skills are either not learned at an adequate rate or do not generalize beyond the narrow teaching setting. To cite a common example, it is useless to work on verbal "yes" and "no" responses at the teaching table and then not to practice at meal times. All you will have is a student who learns to use his skills at the teaching table, and not in the real world setting.

To develop this concept a bit more, I have been involved in literally hundreds of toilet training programs. I cannot, however, toilet train anyone. The best I can do is to get the procedure started and teach others how to follow up for generalization. The student will simply not develop appropriate bladder control unless the program and family keep to the schedule after the intensive "in the bathroom" time. Other students have more than adequate bladder control prior to "training," but do not use the toilet for a myriad of reasons (e.g., ritualistic or attention-seeking behavior). I can "wait the student out" in the bathroom and get him to urinate in the toilet appropriately. Unless others replicate the procedure, however, the effort will have been wasted. Stimulus control will simply develop, and the student's behavior with me will be different than his behavior with others. Successful behavior analysts do not have "magic words" that make behavior occur on cue. It is also not a matter of who the student likes and does not like, or is afraid of or not. There is no magic, and the answer is deceptively simple. Stimulus control is simply a matter of who carries through on well-designed programs and who does not. I am not a guru, and, except when we're trying to lighten the mood, I dislike the common use of that term when referring to behavior analysts. In my opinion, it cheapens the science.

As mentioned above, what people often actually mean when they ask "how many hours of ABA" is "how many hours of Discrete Trial Teaching?" or perhaps more generally "how many hours of 1 to 1 teaching?" This conception misses the point entirely. ABA can be done with large groups of people, and may or may not include 1 to 1 teaching. To return to what will become our key phrase: "IT DEPENDS!" Later in the manual, we will create a hierarchy of general functioning levels and see what sorts of services might be required at each of these functioning levels. We will see that *no one* is too high-functioning to be beyond needing ABA. That goes for those carrying diagnoses and those that we would call typically functioning. Well-designed ABA can teach me new skills, just the same as it can my students. To state it more broadly, I use ABA when I teach my college classes about sex therapy, when I teach my typically developing clients about how to handle anxiety, as well as when I teach my students diagnosed with autism how to speak and interact.

Part of the problem here is the diagnosing of the autistic-spectrum disorders. The diagnostic criteria allow for an enormous functioning range. One student diagnosed with an autistic-spectrum disorder may need quite intensive instruction indeed, both to teach new skills and to manage behavior that is competing with the learning process. Other students may be able to learn and function quite adequately with only minimal extra support, or none at all. While it is true that a student may not require Discrete Trial Teaching, we all require ABA. I need a task analysis to teach me how to fill in the forms the insurance companies ask me to complete for reimbursement. Most often, I give up and simply write the sessions off. If ever a task analysis and empirically verified effective teaching methodologies were needed, it's for me in this situation.

Let's move on to the second statement, which goes something to the effect of "My consultant, Dr. Gimmeitsmine, has described how outdated and oppressive ABA is, and has shown how his system is much better for making the child happy and teaching skills." This is a prime example of the general truism to be careful what you ask for because you just might get it.

When I was first being instructed in ABA by my professors and supervisors, they warned me that ABA would never be popular. ABA wasn't like the other treatments being offered for autism:

1.   It put the onus on the teacher to design programs that would work, rather than blaming the autism ("the student is always right").

2.   It didn't offer a quick fix like other treatments did. This wasn't a shot, or listening to a special sound or even swimming in a tank with a large cetacean. This was hard work, day in and day out for possibly a few years, or possibly a lifetime.

3.   The technique and philosophy require intensive data collection and logical analysis. You don't just "go with your gut," and must approach the subject matter scientifically and objectively.

4.   At times, students might resist the process and not be having any fun (e.g., during an "extinction burst"). In recent yeas, ABA clinicians have developed excellent techniques to address this difficulty.

5.   We had a nasty public image brought about by such popular science fiction books and films as *A Clockwork Orange* and *Brave New World*.

Following the publication of key books within the past decade, most notably those authored or edited by Catherine Maurice, this public image began to change. ABA became what my teachers said it would never become: the most popular kid on the street. The supply of trained people, however, has not kept pace with the demand. For a time, parents and agencies had no means of determining who was a competent practitioner of ABA and who was not. Anyone who so desired could legally print up business cards calling themselves a behavior analyst, or a programmer, or some such similar title. Most frequently, these people would offer parents in-home services, often for cash and off the books. Parents had little to go on in order to ascertain the expertise of those providing services. Most often, word of mouth (a dubious measure at best) was used to decide who was competent and who was not.

In recent years, however, the beginning of a solution has appeared. A certification for behavior analysts has been created, and now there is a standard against which practitioners can be judged. Parents can now ascertain whether the person offering to provide ABA services has the requisite education and properly supervised experience, and has managed to pass the professionally accepted exam that forms the "gold standard" for our profession. This is not a perfect solution, of course. While we would hope that the supervised practice would address this difficulty, the fact remains that I may be able to recite information accurately on a written exam but be completely inept at actually implementing a technique. Still, we are moving in the right direction.

There are currently two levels to this certification: the Board Certified Behavior Analyst and the Board Certified Associate Behavior Analyst. These are now legally controlled terms, and there are very specific levels of education and supervised training that the individual must possess in order to sit for the rigorous examination that all certified behavior analysts of both levels must pass.   Further information can be obtained by visiting the www.bacb.com web page. Interesting trivia point: according to Tom Zane in the newsletter of the New York State Association for Behavior Analysis, David Michael

Newman (15 months old at the time of writing), to whom this book is dedicated, is the first baby on record whose parents are both Board Certified Behavior Analysts. All kidding aside, that should give you an idea of how recent a development this certification is.

Even with this issue solved, however, another has cropped up. This is not what I would call major, but has been made into a very big deal by many people in the field. There are differences in approach and priority for different practitioners. I might begin teaching using an errorless learning system, for example, whereas someone else might begin with a no-no prompting sequence. In reality, this is of course a nonsensical issue within ABA. ABA is an empirical discipline. If the student is not making adequate progress with your system of prompting, you simply switch over to another system. So much for major differences (see also a really brilliant talk given by David Celiberti at the 2001 New York State Association for Behavior Analysis convention for expansion on this idea).

This issue has cropped up in another, more serious form, however. In either an attempt to market an approach, or perhaps actually believing that their approach is truly somehow radically different, some practitioners have begun to claim that what they do is above and beyond "standard" ABA. An example of this at the time of writing is the very hot topic of "verbal behavior." Parents and programs discuss whether or not they do "verbal behavior," as though this was something different from standard ABA practice. The last time I looked, *Verbal Behavior* was a book written by B. F. Skinner in 1957. While it introduces some new vocabulary for the uninitiated, it is by no means outside "standard" ABA. Many of the most famous "standard" ABA programs talk of tacts and mands and other concepts emphasized by those who advocate the focus on verbal behavior. The *Analysis of*

Verbal Behavior journal has been published by, and contributed to, by mainstream behavior analysts for more than a decade. I myself have published in this journal on multiple occasions, as well as other behavioral journals. There was nothing different about the manuscripts I wrote for these different outlets, save the focus of the behavior being worked on.

Gina Green (1996) has provided some excellent criteria for analyzing claims made by programs, whether claiming to be ABA or some other type of treatment. Raymond Romanczyk has added to this in several excellent talks, giving us insight into how to spot quality indicators and how claims that are not tenable regarding treatment are often made. I rely heavily on these two sources as I note just a few of these:

1. Be especially careful of any program where there are no peer-reviewed and published results.

2. Be careful of anywhere where "years of experience" are noted as the criterion of qualification. Thirty years of doing something ineffective is hardly a credential.

3. Be careful of anything where having to *believe* in the system, separate and apart from more overt behavior, is one of the factors that makes the system work.

4. Be careful of claims made based upon an individual having been trained by some famous person, or at some famous place. Unfortunately, not all trainees are equally skilled.

5. Be careful of advocates of systems who avoid peer review but only present their data to lay audiences.

As Grandpa used to say, major scientific breakthroughs are not announced on afternoon talk shows. If a technique stands up to peer-review, there is probably something there. If advocates of a system avoid peer-review, the red warning flags should go up.

Let's provide a "bottom line" analysis as regards ABA programs. If a program is going to "cite the pedigree" of ABA, then programs should adhere to the methodology and philosophy I will describe (see also the "snapshots" describing what ABA is and is not, and the philosophy of ABA in the presentations appendix). Briefly considered, these factors should be:

1.   A commitment to a deterministic philosophy. All behavior occurs for a reason. When we can determine the controlling variables, we can predict the behavior. If we can manipulate the variables, we can shape the behavior.

2.   Data-based decision making. All treatment decisions regarding how teaching should progress are made in keeping with data observed and analyzed (hence the term *"analysis"* in the name of the discipline).

3.   All programs are individualized. There is no such thing as a program that is appropriate for all students. Programs must be baselined and altered in view of the skills the student possesses, the student's learning style, requirements of the environment, the variables governing particular behaviors, etc.

4.   Socially significant behavior is targeted for improvement.

5.   An emphasis on contingencies ("if–> then" relationships between behavior and consequences). We examine A--> B-->C (Antecedent–>Behavior –>Consequence) relationships in order to determine functions of behaviors and therefore to design treatments.

6.   An emphasis on here and now. We are seeking the variables maintaining behavior now, not how the behavior may have been created originally. We constantly collect follow-up data to ensure that programs are having their desired effect. We do not just put a program in place and call it a day. There is constant follow-up and adjustment based upon new data.

7.   An emphasis on reinforcing appropriate behavior ("catch 'em being good"). Aversive or punishing stimuli are avoided.

8.   Observable behavior is used for outcome measures. Results should not be judgment calls, but rather publicly observable improvements.

9.   Learning theory is applied to improve socially significant human behavior.

If any program wishes to call itself an ABA program, it should *at least* meet the criteria stated above (see also other descriptors in presentations appendix and other thoughts presented in such places as Cooper, Heron and Heward's *Applied Behavior Analysis*).

What if a program wishes to say that it somehow goes above and beyond ABA? Quite frankly, I'm not sure how one would go about doing that. How do you go above and beyond an empirical discipline? Was Einstein, a personal hero of mine, no longer doing physics when he created relativity theory? No, what he created is what we would call a "paradigm shift," changing some fundamental assumptions and adding exciting new data. This occurred through the presentation of new findings and new interpretations of old findings in peer-reviewed outlets. We may have new ways of thinking and understanding, but not a new discipline.

Has this type of fundamental paradigm shift occurred with ABA? I think not. If you're considering a system that claims to go above and beyond ABA, you might ask yourself: how do you go above and beyond ABA? Do you not adhere to a deterministic philosophy? Are your decisions regarding treatment not based upon data observed? Are your programs not individualized? Do you not target socially significant behavior? Do you not contingently reinforce socially significant behavior?

It seems to me that all we're talking about is choosing different priorities for programs, some altered prompting strategies, and perhaps different behavioral measures used. That's hardly a reason to come up with a new name or to claim that you have somehow superceded the ABA system. If you invent a new method of reinforcing behavior, it doesn't change the basic laws of reinforcement, or behavior in general. The Graduated ABA that I am outlining is not something outside the realm of "standard" ABA. Neither is Verbal Behavior, nor CABAS™. Neither are approaches that emphasize all incidental teaching, etc. As long as we keep to the criteria stated above, we are comfortably well within the system of ABA that has enjoyed so much clinical success and empirical validation. If we are somehow leaving that discipline, we had better be able to show how we are different and have the empirical data to show how our system is so much better than what has enjoyed massive success for decades. Proponents of the various "schools of thought" that I have mentioned above all share their data at the annual ABA convention. I will refrain from singing *We are Family*, but you get the idea.

Let's turn our attention to the last statement, "We do a modified ABA." Whenever I hear people mention ABA in this manner, I always find myself thinking of that great line from *The Princess Bride*: "You keep on using that word! I do not think it means what you think it means." I have to admit it, I really get bothered by this one. It is often used in a particularly misleading fashion. Parents are told that a school does "modified ABA" and are told that their children will get the benefits of the ABA system as well as the benefits of the other things they do. To understand why this is so dangerous, see sections below on the dangers of intermittent reinforcement. Ask yourself how effective it might be to only take "elements" of the sterilization process that takes place in an operating room, and to leave out other, more troublesome, steps. Often such programs call themselves "eclectic," and it is a very seductive term. "We aren't chained by any particular methodology, we do what works best for each child." Who could argue with that? Actually, I can.

The problem with eclecticism is that there is no consistency during the teaching day, and different educational philosophies suggest very different behavior on the part of the teacher. Let us take the example of a time I was asked to do an emergency consult at a school for children with autistic-spectrum disorders. I was told that the school did "modified ABA," so I was nervous going in.

The boy in question was said to be very aggressive, and this was making teaching impossible. I went to the school to watch staff interact with the child to see if I could determine the variables controlling the aggression. At first, I saw little that I could really say would be at the root of the difficulties. Communication proved to be a particular problem. I saw staff on several occasions changing what they did to communicate with the student, and what type of response they sought from the student. At one point it was a verbal response, at one point a PECS™ symbol, at another point sign language was used. At no time did I see a consistent standard for communication from the student. While troubling, this did not seem to be at the root of the behavior.

After about an hour, the student went off with the physical therapist. Now the rubber hit the road, as it were. The PT took out a puzzle and asked the student to put it together. With a ferocity that would have daunted a wolverine, the student suddenly lunged at the PT, biting and scratching and pulling hair. The PT, to his credit, did not back away and very properly attempted to calm the situation. The student then ran past the PT and it was all I could do to remember that I was there to watch and not intervene just yet.

The "break in the case" came next. The child ran to another part of the room and threw himself down on a pile of mats. I used to believe that I could never be surprised, that I had seen everything there was to see and hear in the field. The next moment changed my mind. As jaded as I am, I was stunned to see the PT stand over the child and say, "Oh, you want to be a pizza!" Sometimes I'm not sure if even as brilliant a novelist as Anne Rice could make some of the things done in the name of autism treatment make sense.

While I wondered what on god's green earth "you want to be a pizza" could possibly mean, wondering if I had somehow transformed into a character in *Memnoch the Devil*, the PT suddenly took an enormous rubber ball and began to roll it up and down the giggling child. This went on for a good minute or two, at which point the child got up and returned to the teaching table. The PT smiled at this development and eagerly followed the child. What followed next was disappointing, but rather easily predictable. The PT took out some clay and asked the student to squeeze it. Again, the student attacked and then ran to the mats. Again, the "you want to be a pizza" ritual was completed. This went on for 45 minutes, at the end of which the PT was quite battered, scratched and bruised. Ten out of ten points for tenacity and style, but minus several thousand for good judgment or training.

As I said above, treatment techniques spring from the philosophy behind the treatment. To a behavior analyst, the contingencies were quite clear: "IF you attack and run to the mats, THEN I will roll this ball on you as you enjoy." When I saw that similar techniques were carried out in the classroom by other staff, the aggression was hardly a mystery.

So why the ball rolling thing? Simply stated, it was suggested by the educational philosophy that some of the staff followed. They believe that a feature of autism is an internal state of physical agitation, a state that can be removed only by providing sensory experiences such as the ball rolling. This particular student had difficulty communicating, as mentioned above. Staff knew that he could not say "please roll the ball on me, I feel internal agitation." So they interpreted his aggression as a nonverbal way of asking for the ball-rolling stimulation.

In no small measure, they were correct. He did indeed attack in order to get the ball. How simple would it have been, however, to teach an alternate way to get the same need met? What if we instead set up a D.R.O. program whereby he got the ball rolling treatment if he *didn't* attack for specified periods? How about giving the student a way to request that is functionally equivalent to aggression, such as a "roll the ball on me" card? Behavior analysts have used such techniques successfully thousands of times. Everybody wins: the student learns a communication skill and gets what he wants, while simultaneously preventing the teacher from getting beaten up.

Consider programs where they might try to combine philosophies, or "be eclectic." The student is engaging in aggression. Why? What do we do? Notice that the ABA and sensory theories suggest radically different treatments. Some approaches to autism suggest that the child should very actively move around the room. Some suggest sitting in a particular place. If a program picks and chooses, or moves from technique to technique during the day, how are students to know which theory staff are following just then and therefore what is expected? Obviously, they can't. Should a student request ball-rolling by aggression or by speaking or using an augmentative communication system? Eclecticism sounds nice, it sounds so American and democratic. Often, however, it is the kiss of death. There is no more a thing called "modified ABA" than there is a thing called "modified pregnancy." You are ABA or you aren't, end of story. I know people are sick of hearing me talk about it, but there is no substitute for the creation of the "culture" of ABA. Whenever I conduct training, that is my primary purpose: to impart the knowledge, philosophy and vocabulary that allows one to become a part of the culture of ABA.

It is crucial that all individuals involved in programming work with a common methodology and vocabulary. As described above, if this is not the case, you may run into trouble when people try to combine fundamentally incompatible models. I find myself thinking of a concept that was ascribed to the comic genius of Marty Feldman. Speaking of comedy, Mr. Feldman said that when writing a skit, internal consistency was the key. Everyone on stage can be holding a duck, and this is accepted without question by the audience. Once the pattern is broken by having an individual walk onto the stage who is NOT carrying a duck, however, you must then explain that and attempt to salvage what was created.

ABA is similar to skit comedy in this respect. You can create various reinforcement contingencies and systems. As long as everyone keeps to the systems, they are simply a fact of life and everything progresses smoothly. If someone violates the model, however, now the whole coherency of the program must be repaired.

It seems that every religion in the world has an axiom that basically amounts to "you can't serve two masters." Whether it be that you cannot love both god and money or this world and heaven as well, it is a truism that you have to follow a particular discipline if you are to be consistent in your behavior. At some point, you need to decide what you want to be when you grow up. If you still want to practice ABA when you grow up, then read on.

This manual is written with the slightly more advanced ABA practitioner in mind, and that certainly includes family members who have been trained in ABA (I draw no distinction between family members and those who do this for a living when it comes to expertise. Both can be equally skilled and knowledgeable). If you do not feel particularly well-grounded in ABA, you might want to skip ahead and begin at chapter four, read through until the end, and then double back to this point. It was not my intention to provide another introductory text, but didn't want this manual to be unfriendly to those who require more introductory material. The compromise was to provide what I hope is a nice outline from an earlier introductory training manual written a few years ago.

Chapter Two: What Level of Intensity?

Let's begin by breaking ABA down into two efforts that are engaged in simultaneously:

1.   Teaching new skills, particularly learning-to-learn skills.

2.   Reducing behaviors that are interfering with learning (what Ira Cohen calls "competing behavior").

We can break our work down into levels, but please do not misinterpret these somehow as developmental stages. They are merely a convenient way of breaking down functioning levels typically encountered when working with students diagnosed with autistic-spectrum disorders. Some students may begin at the beginning, other students may begin with a later level.

The three factors that characterize the different levels are:

1.   What new skills should we attempt to teach?

2.   What teaching strategies (including level of intensity and presence of other students) should we employ?

3.   What behavior management strategies (including types of consequences and schedule) should we utilize?

As we look at the different levels, the differences across functioning levels will become more obvious. What we are really dealing with is a continuum, going from a very carefully contrived teaching situation to one that as closely as possible approximates normal, everyday situations. Finally, when no special teaching is needed, the student returns to mainstream environments with his/her typically developing peers.

One might ask why we must initially contrive situations in order to teach. Won't we then have to work our way back to normalized situations? The objection is well-taken, but I believe a little careful examination answers the question. Consider the issue of reinforcer selection. The use of primary (e.g., food) reinforcers is very common when one first begins teaching children diagnosed with autistic-spectrum disorders (although always paired with social reinforcement such as praise). These give way to more social and generalized (token) reinforcers, and then finally to the everyday social consequences that characterize typical interactions.

We must answer the questions posed above. Why not simply begin with the everyday social consequences alone? Wouldn't that be more normalizing and then we wouldn't have to fade back from the contrived situation towards normal interactions? It is a fair question, but one with a very simple answer: for many students, beginning with social praise alone as a reinforcer would be useless. If a student, because of his/her social difficulties, does not find praise particularly reinforcing then it is useless to give social praise alone. There would be no behavior-altering effect of the praise.

Remember, not all consequences are reinforcers, regardless of intent. Praise is only a reinforcer if its contingent delivery increases the future probability of the behavior that preceded it. If this is not the case, praise is *simply not yet a reinforcer*. We will have to teach this social interest, and have the person come to value our praise (e.g., Sidman, 1989). All praise is not created equal. I find Don Imus interesting and his literary criticism valuable. If, however, I flipped around the radio channels and found one of the New York "shock jocks" praising one of my previous books, I would immediately have it pulled from the shelves. I would know I had done something wrong.

Reinforcers are, after all, very individualized. I sometimes work with a speech therapist who is one of the most skilled clinicians I have ever known. I don't, however, share her interest in some of the "reality television" programs, or understand what is even vaguely interesting about them. She and I were doing some work together in England when their *Big Brother* show came on. The whole country seemed to come to a standstill to watch. I sat and stared in disbelief with David Carr of the English parents' group F.A.I.T.H. (Focusing on Autism In The Home). He summed it up beautifully, "I'd rather knock out my teeth with a hammer than watch that." I could not agree more and stepped out into the cool night air to smoke a cigar. I found myself thinking of my colleague's keen interest in that *Survivor* television program. I tried to watch it once and found myself wishing that the army would conduct nuclear testing on the island. My boredom aside, millions of people found the show riveting and very reinforcing (obviously a sure sign that society is spiraling towards its end). Why can't people watch quality programs like *Ray Bradbury Theater* or *Get Smart*? We watch a lot of *Sesame Street* in my house. My mother-in-law Lucille loves Rosita, a very happy muppet who does a lot of hugging. My wife is partial to Grover, my mom likes Kermit, my son loves Elmo, and I'm an Oscar the Grouch man. I still believe that one of the funniest lines in the history of television came during a sing-along on *Sesame Street*. Oscar exclaimed something to the effect of "Oh no, my worst nightmare! I'm in the middle of a heartfelt anthem!" It doesn't get any better than that for showing the individuality of reinforcers.

Consider now the specially designed teaching situation. Why go through the trouble? Why not simply sit the student in a classroom of typically developing children and have him learn as the other students do? Perhaps a bit of a case study can answer that question.

I was asked to do a consultation at a school in central New York State. There were behavioral difficulties being demonstrated by a particular student, and the school was not able to ameliorate the situation. Finally, after considerable pressure on the school from the student's mother, I was asked to come and visit and provide consultation.

I couldn't clear the necessary time on my schedule for three months. The ABA convention was coming up, and I was scheduled to speak in Canada a week after that. Problem solved. I would speak at the ABA convention, come home just long enough to change suitcases, pop up to the school and then on to Canada. After the plans were made, my wife became pregnant with our wonderful son. Her first sonogram was scheduled for the week I would be traveling, consulting and lecturing. I was now going to miss it. We landed after the ABA convention and two hours later Dana drove me back to the airport, with the Harry Chapin song *Cats in the Cradle* repeating endlessly in my head. I felt like the worst person alive.

When I arrived at the school, my mood did not improve. I was shown to the student's class. I have to admit, at first glance the class looked awesome. There were three or four students who seemed somewhat lower functioning, but this was a kindergarten class of children with autism who seemed as typically functioning as any I had ever seen. There was a simple explanation for that. This *was* a class of typically developing children. In this school district, they didn't believe in separating students with disabilities and thus the four students diagnosed with autism were enrolled in the class of typically developing children, with two staff assigned to them.

A ratio of two children to one staff member is certainly not a bad one. The problem soon became evident, however. The needs of two of the children were such that they required 1 to 1 assistance during nearly all activities. The other two children diagnosed with autism did a good bit of wandering. I was told that this full inclusionary philosophy was not just for the kindergarten, but for all grade levels. While I pondered the awesome implications, we moved to the cafeteria. It was time to rehearse for the school pageant.

"Great moments in fairy tales" was the theme. I watched in morbid fascination as the children diagnosed with autism were dressed as "all the king's horses." A little wry reflection provided the explanation: horses don't have lines to recite. I then watched in more than morbid fascination as the children were physically prompted (practically needing to be shoved) across the stage. Three of the children ripped at their costumes as this went on, possibly due to tactile defensiveness issues or possibly due to the obsessive-compulsive qualities sometimes seen with children diagnosed with autistic-spectrum disorders. The other activities of the school day seemed equally lost on at least two of the students. I find myself thinking of a story I heard Caroll Spiney (the performer behind Oscar the Grouch and Big Bird on *Sesame Street*) tell. The great Jim Henson had watched a rather difficult audition and had commented "I really like what you were trying to do!" The idea was great, but it just didn't work out in actual practice.

Please don't get me wrong. I am a huge fan of mainstreaming and have personally designed programs for school districts to help children diagnosed with autistic-spectrum disorders to participate in classes with their typically-developing peers. I do, however, believe in helping students to first develop the pre-requisite skills that will allow them to be successful in these mainstream settings. Otherwise, it is akin to taking a child who cannot speak and announcing that (s)he will not get lunch until (s)he asks for it in a full sentence. Such a "tough-minded" stance might be appropriate at some point when the student has developed the pre-requisite skills. Prior to that, however, one is dealing with illusions and possibly even cruelty.

Why the need for the specifically designed learning opportunities? The issue comes down to one of learning style and the nature of the disabilities that we call the autistic-spectrum disorders. A wide variety of names and descriptions have been given to characterize the ways in which children with autism may have difficulties in processing information. I will not repeat that information here, but rather refer the reader to some excellent works listed in the suggested reading section at the conclusion of the manual. We can mention a few of the main issues:

1.   Students diagnosed with autistic-spectrum disorders are often described as very easily distracted by ambient stimuli (even a piece of dust floating in the peripheral vision may be sufficient to draw attention away from a speaker).

2.   Students diagnosed with autistic-spectrum disorders may engage in behavior that interferes with their attention to others (e.g., perseverative humming or singing that distracts from the teaching situation).

3.   Students diagnosed with autistic-spectrum disorders may have auditory processing problems such that it is difficult for them to "screen out" ambient noise.

4.   Students diagnosed with autistic-spectrum disorders may be unduly distracted by, or "hone in" on, irrelevant aspects of a stimulus (e.g., concentrating on the color of a dollar bill, rather than the numbers or picture on it).

5.   Students diagnosed with autistic-spectrum disorders may be unable to follow spoken directions without intensive training.

6.   Students diagnosed with autistic-spectrum disorders may be unable to imitate language or actions without intensive training.

All of this is simply to say that children diagnosed with autistic-spectrum disorders may have great difficulty in focusing on, and gaining information from, spoken conversation and other typical ways of presenting information. Unfortunately, most teaching in mainstream programs is provided in this manner. How are these students to learn in mainstream settings? Obviously, it would be difficult if not impossible.

I am going to break student functioning down into *very broad* categories. This is merely for explanation purposes, and not to suggest these are the only levels we could conceptualize. We could probably make 20 finer gradations than I will make. I am merely attempting to show how one might begin to approach programming in a graduated fashion. As we look at the levels, we will have to consider the three programming factors outlined at the beginning of the chapter:

1.   What new skills should we attempt to teach?

2.   What teaching strategies (including level of intensity and presence of other students) should we employ?

3.   What behavior management strategies (including types of consequences and schedule) should we utilize?

I will be providing sample teaching programs for each level. What I will provide is only the tip of the proverbial iceberg. There are literally thousands of programs one would work on over the course of a student's time in program. This plethora of programs is detailed in some excellent resources. I prefer Raymond Romanczyk Individual Goal Selection (I.G.S.) Curriculum and would direct the reader there for much more elaboration.

Please remember that what I am presenting are *general* levels and *sample* programs and teaching strategies to give a general idea of what I mean by graduated ABA. Other clinicians might create other equally valid hierarchies, and might locate particular programs or teaching strategies in levels different from mine. That is not the point;

I am merely trying to present one model and to demonstrate the idea of a graduated model of ABA.

It must also always be remembered that students will, of course, not always fit exactly into levels. To return to an earlier example, while many level one students do not typically find social praise reinforcing, some students do. As always, programs are individualized, as is the hallmark of ABA. For some reason, for example, it might also be appropriate to teach a more advanced skill earlier (e.g., teaching turn-taking in a family with several siblings closely spaced in age). Standardized tests that provide age-norms may provide additional suggestions.

An additional philosophical point that bears mentioning is that students should be provided with as much choice as humanly possible when teaching. Too much of life simply "happens" to students and they have no say over what is going on. Why must this be the case? If you are going to work on two different programs, does it matter which you do first? Not generally. Therefore, why not let the student pick (either verbally or by pointing at a visual representation of the program) the order? Why not let the student choose the reinforcers to be earned? How about letting the student choose teaching stimuli? Increasing student choice-making will tend to cut down quite a bit on student resistance, and make sessions more pleasant for all concerned (e.g., Newman, Needelman, Reinecke, & Robek, in press).

Two final points bear mentioning. Individual programs should be instituted as soon as the student is ready. These "levels" are just for demonstration purposes. In other words, if a student is ready for a verbal "yes/no" program, don't wait until other programs catch up to institute the program.

It is also a crucial practice to make communication as functional as possible as soon as possible. While I locate the "requesting" program in level two, for example, it is good clinical practice to start working on this at the earliest opportunity. If a child is able to "mand," their communication will be functional and will likely be maintained in the behavioral repertoire. I always recommend trying to shape vocalizations as soon as possible, accepting crude approximations at first and shaping the verbalizations to become more and more appropriate. We have to remember that speaking, for whatever reason, is difficult for many students with autism. To make the effort worth their while, speaking has to help the child to negotiate and manipulate (in the nicest sense) their world. Simple sounds can become requests, labels, greetings, or other verbal skills with just a little careful shaping.

Level One

Skills to teach: we are dealing here at the most basic level. We will need to teach the basics of attending to another individual for a sufficient length of time to carry on a simple "one exchange" interaction. Typical programs at this point include eye to face contact, following one step directives, one step motor imitation, simple verbal imitation, matching, and receptive object identification. Basic self-help skills such as toileting, dressing, and feeding may need to be addressed. In the very earliest interactions, one may not try to teach anything at all, but rather practice skills that students already possess, so as to make for easy success and therefore ample reinforcement. Do not be afraid to use noncontingent reinforcement for a time as well (see below). Also keep an eye out for where "functionally equivalent" behaviors can be taught in order to reduce inappropriate behavior (e.g., the use of a card with "I need a break" written on it being used instead of the student attacking a teacher or engaging in self-injurious behavior. The student need not be able to read to make such programs work, only to associate the action of giving the card with the consequence of getting a break).

Teaching strategies: this is most often done through standard discrete trial teaching as defined in its own chapter below. Often, as distraction-free a setting as possible is necessary, as well as fairly simple language that eliminates unnecessary words within sentences. While cues should be varied somewhat to increase probability of generalization, excessive language should be avoided. Task analyses of self-help skills are designed and taught, in keeping with the techniques of shaping, chaining, and prompt fading. Visual prompting strategies may be combined with verbal cues (e.g., holding up a picture of an item as you make a verbal request for the student to touch the actual object in a receptive object identification program).

Behavior management strategies: A student at this level may display a great many behaviors that compete with the learning process. Based upon a functional analysis of these competing behaviors, treatment plans need to be drawn up accordingly. Typical programs include extinction of avoidance behavior and reinforcement of the absence of such behavior (for example through the use of a Differential Reinforcement of Other behavior program). Reinforcement is typically immediate and often makes use of primaries paired with social praise. Do not hesitate to use a great deal of noncontingent reinforcement in the very earliest stages of interaction, trying to establish oneself as a reinforcer. You may use very descriptive praise (e.g., "Good sitting") at this stage. Remember that the student may not understand social interactions and may not know what you mean by "good job." What are you praising? The good direction-following? Good posture? Good even breathing rates? By being descriptive in your praise, you may eliminate confusion relative to more ambiguous phrasing.

Augmentative communication systems are used by some practitioners in this and other early levels. If a student does not have a means of communication, one may observe the student engaging in a great deal of "inappropriate" behavior that actually serves a communicative function (e.g., Carr & Durand, 1985). As mentioned above, teaching functionally equivalent communication responses can eliminate much inappropriate behavior.

Level Two

Skills to teach: we can now make programs a bit more sophisticated. Length of attention can be increased and minor distracting stimuli may be purposely employed to make it more challenging for the student to attend. Programs start to become more complex. One step directives become two step directives. One step motor imitation becomes two step and the imitation skills can be used to teach functional skills such as appropriate toy play. Matching programs gradually give way to categorization. Verbal imitation gives way to labels, requests, yes/no, greetings, etc. as verbal approximations develop and are shaped.

Teaching strategies: while standard discrete trial teaching is often employed here, a real focus has to be made on generalizing the skills into everyday environments. Verbal approximations must be used in everyday interactions. To elaborate the example given above, if a student has developed the ability to use a verbal yes and no, even if they are only understandable approximations, then they must be used at meal-times before meals are presented (see section in chapter one on generalization). If that means that there is a two hour wait for dinner, that is what it comes to at times. Add in more distracting stimuli. Vary cues and make sure to vary teaching stimuli widely as well (e.g., use crayons, papers, toy cars, colored clay, etc. to teach a concept of a color and not always the same stimulus such as colored "swatches"). Some additional language can be thrown in to make more normalized interactions (e.g., adding in "please" or "would you" to requests, in order to increase language and distractions). Teaching tends to still be fairly teacher-directed at this point. As advocated very effectively by Dr. Vicki Sudhalter, make sure to work on "concepts" rather than just responses. If doing a receptive body-part identification drill, have the student point to his/her nose, the teacher's nose and a doll's nose (this way the student knows the general concept of noses and doesn't think that only that bump on his/her face is *named* nose). If necessary, continue to use visual prompting strategies (e.g., hold up a red piece of paper as you ask the student to pick the color red in a receptive color identification program). Systematically fade these out when possible. Make sure to remember to work on teaching the student appropriate leisure skills. A common issue for parents is that students can not be constructively occupied for even a few minutes without supervision. Also, if a student does not possess any leisure skills, (s)he may engage in inappropriate behavior when not otherwise occupied. In such cases, it is very important to teach leisure skills such as block building, drawing, coloring, computer games, etc.

Behavior management strategies: As always, a functional analysis of competing behaviors must be conducted and treatment plans need to be drawn up accordingly. Reinforcers should start to become more normalized, with primaries becoming more intermittent and social praise taking more of the center stage. You may still use good, descriptive praise. Try to begin fading in some more normal phrasing as well on some trials, however, teaching students that these are equivalent phrases.

Level Three

Skills to teach: programming gets into finer gradations and more and more information (e.g., comparative concepts, quantity concepts, pronouns and prepositions, statements of personal information, simple conversational exchanges, basic pre-academics, interactive play programs, etc.) Programs should begin to aim at having *the student make the initiation in an interaction*. Rather than the staff initiating a greeting, staff might enter a room and establish eye contact and wait for the student to make the greeting (sometimes using a second instructor to prompt, but fading this as quickly as possible). Staff might play with a favorite toy and wait for the student to make a request to play along. We sometimes play with toys in bags, making a big show of it and thereby eliciting students to come over and ask what we are doing. Watch very carefully to fade questions such as "what do you want" from requesting programs and try to use more visual prompting strategies as we fade towards normalization. Require longer length of utterances by teacher and students.

Teaching strategies: standard discrete trial teaching should fade towards a combination of discrete trial and more incidental teaching approaches. The emphasis is on creating situations whereby the student will spontaneously use the skills worked on in 1 to 1 teaching. We must attempt to step up the focus on generalizing skills into everyday environments. Take the prepositions and pronoun programs to the park and work on them with other children and park equipment. "Stage" and script out common interactive scenarios. Bring other children into the home and practice play and turn-taking and other socially appropriate skills. Whenever possible, use everyday language and avoid special phrasing unless absolutely necessary during teaching time. Have students initiate as much activity as possible, using appropriate language. In school settings, make sure to start working on group learning exercises. Try to fade extra prompting strategies, such as any physical prompting, if at all possible. Don't forget to work on skills one would need in a school setting (e.g., lining up, hanging up a coat in the closet, finding one's possessions, etc.).

Behavior management strategies: as always, a functional analysis of competing behaviors must be conducted and treatment plans need to be drawn up accordingly. Reinforcers should begin to take the form of a generalized system (e.g., a token economy, see "how to set up a token economy" in the chapter on conceptualizing behavior). Tokens are earned on a fairly dense schedule, and are traded in several times during a session. Praise should become almost conversational, with some descriptive elements but largely everyday conversation. Rudimentary contingency contracting may become possible.

Level Four

Skills to teach: programming should stop focusing on the transmission of information alone, and really emphasize more advanced social and language programs. An emphasis should be placed on appropriate play in group settings. Language should largely take the form of student initiations and much more advanced and free-flowing conversation.

Teaching strategies: small group instruction is the rule of this stage. Any 1 to 1 should really be saved for skills that are particularly lagging. The "staged" interactions of the prior level should give way to actual spontaneous exchanges in the settings in which the skills would have to be displayed if the child were typically developing (because, in truth, s/he is getting to the point of being able to function in real-world settings with minimal support). Avoid special phrasing unless absolutely necessary during teaching time. Have students initiate as much activity as possible, using appropriate language.

Behavior management strategies: as always, a functional analysis of competing behaviors must be conducted and treatment plans need to be drawn up accordingly. Reinforcement systems should take the form of both short-term and long-term token economies (see "how to set up a token economy" in the chapter on conceptualizing behavior). Tokens are earned on a fairly dense schedule during program time, but on a leaner schedule for general behavior management and goal completion outside of session time. Language, including praise, should become largely everyday conversation. Self-management training (see below) should commence.

Level Five

Skills to teach: a standardized curriculum of preschool and school instruction should be followed, based upon the child's chronological age and achievement to this point. Any lagging social, play and conversational skills should be practiced intensively.

Teaching strategies: larger group instruction in a normalized manner is the rule of this stage, with any 1 to 1 avoided unless particularly needed to address severely lagging skills.

Behavior management strategies: at this stage, reinforcement systems should take the form of primarily long-term token economies to encourage appropriate learning and behavior as would be seen in a well-structured mainstream classroom.

Level Six

No special help necessary on any level. The individual can choose the learning style necessary to acquire information. That is, the person can evaluate and adapt to a new learning environment at a reasonable rate so as to not miss the train of information passing by. Note to student at this point: have a good life. Don't waste time being concerned with actors and singers and athletes.

Self-management

As a capsule version of what one might see as one moves through the levels, let's look at self-management training. See the chapter on self-management below, but suffice to say for the moment that self-management training is highly desirable in terms of helping the student to require far less behavior management assistance from a teacher and therefore to greatly increase independence.

I, along with some really wonderful colleagues, have published some studies of teaching self-management skills to children diagnosed with autism over the past few years. The studies have examined how students with autism could do such things as increase their appropriate conversation, sharing skills, behavioral variability, and decrease inappropriate behavior by learning good self-management skills (see reference section below).

We conceptualize self-management training as a three stage process:

1. *Externally-delivered reinforcement*: This is your standard teaching arrangement. The teacher prompts responses, judges accuracy of responses, and delivers reinforcers based upon student performance.

2.   *Prompted self-reinforcement*: Here, the teacher begins to fade his/her presence. Rather than delivering reinforcers, the teacher might prompt the student to take his/her tokens. During the early portions of this stage, one tells students when they have performed skills accurately and reminds them to take reinforcers. Later, one asks questions (e.g., "You got it right, what should you do?"). Finally, staff fade their prompts entirely and the student must remember to judge his/her own behavior and reinforce or not accordingly. As one sees this self-monitoring and self-reinforcement being done more and more accurately, it becomes apparent that the student is ready for stage three.

3.   *Self-management*: In this last stage, the student is solely responsible for self-monitoring and self-reinforcement.

My favorite bit of video footage from my clinical library deals with just such a progression. I sit down with a student to do simple arithmetic examples. He was perfectly capable of doing the examples, but was highly prompt-dependent. He would do one example on a sheet and then wait for someone to tell him to do the next one. It was a perfect time for self-management training.

We began with straight-forward externally-delivered reinforcement. This worked very well, as he was getting all the prompting and reinforcement he needed. As we moved into prompted self-reinforcement, the child began to mimic my voice and phrasing as he worked, filling the gaps as I was fading my presence. Finally, the last section of tape shows him doing completely independent self-management. He sat alone in the room doing his worksheets, mimicking my voice and reinforcement and even how I sometimes twirl my pen in my hands in between tasks. He's one of the world's cutest guys and it always gets a great reaction from audiences. He's back at mainstream program now, minus the overt vocalizations as he self-manages. As an interesting footnote on self-management, we have seen in our studies that children diagnosed with autism are much less likely to cheat and take reinforcers they don't deserve than are typically developing students.

As a concluding note on this section, I cannot emphasize enough the need to work towards more normalized teaching as one moves along. In the past few years, I have found myself doing many evaluations of student progress at the request of both families and school districts. A tremendous problem has surfaced due to a tendency to work in too restricted a fashion.

Many students have received so much intensive drilling in a 1 to 1 setting that they cannot function in any other type of setting; introduce even one other student into the setting and the student ceases to display skills. He simply has not been taught to process multiple variables or to adapt to environmental changes. We do students a disservice when we do not teach them to function in more typical learning settings.

Another issue deals with the selection of teaching stimuli. Programmers believe the child has mastered the concept of "red," but only the same colored piece of construction paper has ever been used to teach the color. He doesn't know the color red, he thinks that piece of paper is *named* red! Take out a red crayon or clay and he cannot label it.

Another problem deals with phrasings. I have, for example, conducted standardized IQ tests for students and used the phrasing required by the testing manual. Someone quickly jumps up and says "No, you can't ask it like that! You have to say 'touch' because he doesn't know 'point to' or 'where is' or 'show me' or 'give me the', etc." They then tell me that I must reinforce success on every item or the student will lose interest. I explain that the standardization of some tests requires very precise scripting, and many tests do not allow for such reinforcement. We acknowledge the difficulties together and agree that scores will probably not be anything even vaguely resembling a true measure of the student's ability.

Obviously, in these cases, programming did a serious disservice to the child. We have bought "100 percent correct" on the graph at the cost of actually teaching the student how to demonstrate skills in a real world setting. This student will score in the delayed range of intellectual functioning, not due to any real intellectual deficit, but due to the peculiar teaching. Bottom line: generalization into typical settings, stimuli and speech cannot be expected or prayed for. It must be encouraged through appropriate programming. There will not be what I have called in my darker moments "1 to 1 valets" available at all times for the student. _Absolutely give them the 1 to 1 if they need it in the beginning, but there had better be one heck of an intensive effort going on to help the student develop skills so that they no longer need that level of help in perpetuity._

Chapter Three: The AMAC Graduated ABA Model

Bobby Newman and Frederica Blausten

Since joining AMAC in 1995 as Director of Training and Research, I (BN) have seen the marked progression of children within this graduated model.   This program has implemented a continuum of services that "graduates" children from an extremely intensive model to one that emphasizes more typical instruction.   The programs, preschool since 1992 and school-age since 1995, were created by Executive Director Frederica Blausten ("Rica") and address the range of needs typically displayed by students diagnosed with autistic-spectrum disorders.   This is a trans-disciplinary model wherein the Principal of the school, Ellice Geller (who is also a speech therapist) draws together all disciplines to provide instruction within the ABA model.   By having the program offer three different intensities of services, AMAC facilitates learning across the functioning spectrum. The options are:

1.   Six students, one teacher and three teacher assistants (6:1+3). These are known as Special Needs Units (SNU).

2.   Eight students, one teacher and two teacher assistants (8:1+2). These are known as Communication and Augmentative Needs (CAN).

3.   Ten students, one teacher and one teacher assistant (10:1+1), the Team 10 classes.

In all cases, the staffing ratios mentioned above are supplemented by related service providers as mandated on student IEP's. Related services are provided on a "push in" system, with the services being delivered within the classroom itself. That's where the skills need to be demonstrated first, so we teach there first (while of course programming for generalization).

This issue of "related service" providers has been a controversial one within ABA circles. Let's take a side trip to explore it. Many within the ABA tradition have had a great deal of difficulty dealing with the role of related service providers within their schools and programs. "Behavior is behavior," some ABA people reason. Why do we need specialists such as speech therapists and occupational therapists to address particular programmatic areas?

On the surface, this objection seems valid and I would be lying if I said I hadn't found myself compelled by the logic at many points during my career. Are related service providers really necessary at our programs? Meredith Needelman and I attempted to get away from the political battles over this question and set out to examine this question from an empirical standpoint.

We designed a study whereby we examined how quickly students diagnosed with autism would acquire verbal skills, based upon level of speech therapist involvement in programmatic design and implementation (Newman & Needelman, 2000, see also a summary in Needelman, 2000). Our results were intriguing. The inclusion or absence of a speech therapist had no effect on the students' skill acquisition. Score one for the forces that claim related services are an unnecessary expense and personnel burden.

The results of our study may be misleading, however. The programs that were targeted for teaching were all fairly standard and were well-known to the teaching staff. In fact, at AMAC, all staff are taught to implement programs regardless of domains. If we had chosen to examine more unfamiliar programs, or if complications had arisen during teaching, the speech therapist might have proven necessary. Planned studies will address these issues. At AMAC, Rica has required that all therapists write programs in their area of specialty and then teach the staff how to carry out these programs. The cross-training naturally provides the trans-disciplinary approach described above.

One particular evening, though, helped settle the issue in my (BN's) mind and to realize the importance of some specialists. A speech therapist had asked me to watch programming with a child who was also involved in a home program. The consultant overseeing the program was making what we both regarded as some questionable recommendations. I watched to provide a fresh set of eyes.

I watched the speech therapist working with the child. I was struck when the child reached for some juice and the speech therapist prompted, "Oh, you want juice! Duh duh duh juice." At the risk of demonstrating my ignorance or incomplete training, that seemed odd to me and I assumed it was one of the questionable recommendations the home programmer had made.

During a break, I asked "what's up with the duh duh thing?" The speech therapist didn't look up from her graphing. "Duh is a sound many children learn before juh. 'Duh' is a part of the 'juh' sound, so we sometimes go for that first." I wasn't sure if she was taking me seriously, so I responded in kind.

"You're making that up."

At that point she looked up at me, trying to ascertain if I was serious.

"You didn't know that?"

"Nope. I've taught several hundred kids to say juice and as god is my witness, I have *never* heard that you should teach them to say 'duh' first."

She patiently explained the oral motor mechanics to me, and I began to realize that while I had successfully taught more kids to say "juice" than I could remember, perhaps I hadn't been doing it as efficiently as possible. Thus, a speech therapist's knowledge of the mechanics of sound production could have shaved a great deal of teaching time and effort. When guided by sound behavioral principles, there is a place for well-trained related service professionals. ABA has some amazing teaching technologies. A little crucial knowledge from outside the discipline, however, helps us to know *what* to teach.

AMAC uses this developmental knowledge, often not taught in behavioral circles, to choose what to teach next. Rica has brought in the curriculum used at SUNY Binghamton by Dr. Raymond Romanczyk as the basic structure of curriculum choice. The AMAC model encourages all disciplines to choose what to teach based upon proven guidelines, developmentally-based when these are empirically supported. Thus, the therapist's classic choice of "DUH DUH" is an attempt to provide a learning opportunity that has a high probability of success. Developmentally speaking, most children learn the "duh" sound first. If such an approach did not work, however, she, as all good behaviorists, would try other approaches. A more traditional therapist, not following such a data-based decision-making model, might continue to simply prompt "duh" even when this strategy proved unsuccessful. As Rica suggested when we discussed the case, if it still didn't work, perhaps the child simply doesn't find juice reinforcing and we should try milk or soda!

Anyway, back to the graduated model. Students are placed into classes upon entry to the AMAC program, based primarily upon the extent to which the students require 1 to 1 teaching in order to learn new skills and to reduce competing behavior, and consequently their ability to learn within a larger group. While it is generally the case that students in the classes with the lower staff to student ratios have mastered basic skills and self-help issues, this is not always the case. The basic rule of "assume nothing" when it comes to students diagnosed with autistic-spectrum disorders holds. It is not unusual for a student to have mastered relatively complex skills, often via rote or exact imitation, and yet still have deficits in some area of self-help such as toileting or feeding. An AMAC student in a class of six students may be able to speak, but does not initiate in new settings. An AMAC student in a class of eight students generally has developed verbal skills, or is using an augmentative communication system such as PECS™ to spontaneously make choices.

The key issue in placement is the ability to learn within larger groups. Here we recognize the importance of the ability to learn in different sized groups and varied environments. Learning from environmental stimuli, your neighbor, the other adults, and in random settings reduces dependence on one person or one expected prompt. When a child in a class of six sits together at group-supervised lunch and shows curiosity about the goodies another student has, making initiations and accepting same, we know he's moving along towards being able to function in less restrictive environments. (S)he will be able to learn from more of a typical presentation style (provided we have also addressed the behavior management needs of the individual).

With the issues of prompt dependency, generalization and transitioning into mainstream settings detailed in our last chapter firmly in mind, students are moved through the hierarchy of classes as soon as they are able to learn in larger groups, and then finally returned to less restrictive settings. As detailed by Judith Favell in a particularly wonderful talk she gave to the New York State Association for Behavior Analysis (NYSABA, Inc.) a few years ago, students must be prepared for life in the group community. By limiting instruction to 1 to 1, our pupils would fall behind. Expecting that there will always be 1 to 1 assistance in "the real world" is unrealistic. We have to be sure to teach students to learn in more normalized environments, which fosters independence.

Often, students come to the AMAC program requiring intensive 1 to 1 instruction in order to maximize gains and to manage behavior. They therefore begin in the classes of six students, where the vast majority of the day is spent on 1 to 1 teaching. It must be noted that while this often means discrete trial teaching, it need not take that form. We have seen that some students learn more easily in a more incidental format (Newman, Lyttle, & Bohonos, 2000). As one tours the AMAC facility, one will find staff walking around the building with students, taking advantage of pre-arranged opportunities to practice skills. This more incidental teaching is done in no less rigorous a fashion, with staff collecting data just as they do during the "sit down" 1 to 1 time. Staff can be quite ingenious as they covertly take data on these learning opportunities. It is not unusual for staff to go out for lunch and to realize that they have some masking tape on their inner arms that details a student's fluency with making greetings or labeling numbers that have been planted on walls and doors. This data is of course transferred to more formalized record keeping systems during afternoon meetings.

Even in the classes of six students, however, there are some group lessons and opportunities for generalizing skills to the group setting. Motor imitation learned in 1 to 1 time is practiced during physical education. Requests practiced during 1 to 1 are generalized to "family style" lunches and snacks. Staff are careful to systematically fade prompts, and as we see that students are able to demonstrate their skills and acquire new ones in the group setting, we know they are ready to move on into less restrictive environments.

In all classes, work is individualized for the students based upon baseline observations of skills and analysis of subsequent data regarding skill acquisition. It is therefore much more the rule than the exception for group lessons to be structured according to individual needs. A group of students working on money skills might see one student working on identifying bills and coins, while another works on the values, while another works on calculating tax and making change.

Similarly, behavior management programs are often "the same but different." In addition to individualized behavior management programs, there are AMAC systems that go throughout all programs. There are intensive and immediate reinforcement systems in place, using classic samples and intervals. In addition, the Reward Store is an institution at AMAC. This is an over-riding token economy that features a massive inventory that either travels to reach each student personally throughout the building, or children and staff can visit a well-equipped general store with everything from ice cream to the latest magazines. The Reward Store was designed by Rica to increase the density of reinforcement and, as is required for all staff, is a way for administration to ensure that positive reinforcement is agency-wide. At several regularly scheduled intervals during the day, students receive various forms of tokens (ranging from bracelets to AMAC dollar bills) that can be exchanged for commodities or favored activities from a roving cart or a central store location. The bills were created as some of us couldn't sleep one night at summer camp a few years ago. We had the one dollar "Sherall," the five dollar "Sarah" and such. Rica made the very sensible suggestion that we take the "In Bobby We

Trust" off the bills and replace it with the AMAC slogan, "A Family of Services."   She didn't want anyone to accuse me of being a megalomaniac, whatever that is ☺

The Reward Store shows the individualization that can be built into such a system. Parents and guardians are queried regularly for possible inventory items. Some students, generally those who would be described as lower functioning, trade in their tokens immediately for toys and primary reinforcers and favored activities. Some students save their tokens for big ticket items such as fairly expensive toys. One particularly enterprising student saved large numbers of tokens for video-tapes of the professional wrestling shows. I would watch the shows live with my father-in-law and tape them for the student to see (with his parents' permission, and he would return them after viewing so that we did not violate copyright laws). He chose to save tokens for two weeks at a time in order to earn these tapes. I really liked this last example of the reward store in action, as it was not specifically the wrestling the student was interested in. Rather, the other children in the neighborhood would be talking about what happened the prior evening on the show, and he would feel left out if he did not know what had happened. He would take the tape home and quickly fast forward through it so he could learn the latest plot lines in the never-ending drama and know what had happened. He could then happily discuss it when other children asked, "did you see when…." That kind of social interest is what we have been shooting for all along, and it's always gratifying to see it.

Such events are a reminder of the social skills and social interest we are attempting to help students develop. I personally find it a bit annoying when students argue and fight. It seems that every dispute, in the final analysis, boils down to who "dissed" (showed disrespect towards) who. Think about it, though. Once upon a time, most such students did not display any social interest. Now there is massive concern over social status and positive perceptions from others. I'd call that a major accomplishment. These are the students who have moved to the classes of 8 or 10 and are learning to negotiate with a peer. This is not something a 1 to 1 shadow in the mainstream can teach easily. At AMAC, students are graduating up the ladder (see cover design!) to speak for themselves.

Interestingly, I find that many parents are hesitant to have students move from the classes with the higher staff to student ratios to the classes with lower staff to student ratios. At first glance, you would think that such a move, which is indicative of major strides by the student, would be cause for major celebration. The very success we have seen, however, is the reason for the concern. "If it ain't broke, don't fix it" seems to be the guiding philosophy. If a student is making so much progress with the intensive intervention, why should we alter it? I have to admit, I used to be surprised by the apprehension that accompanied my suggestion that the student move on. In retrospect, I suppose it is understandable but also demonstrates what I regard as a dangerous fallacy.

This idea that more 1 to 1 is better than less is indeed a dangerous one. As argued in the previous chapter, this can often lead to great prompt dependency, and a complete inability to function in a group environment. There is a misconception that more 1 to 1 time means greater intensity of instruction. It does not. One can be every bit as rigorous in larger group instruction. The key is still the data-based decision making and teaching technique selection. There is no less rigor within the larger groups. Of course, students should only move into the larger groups as they have developed the skills (social, behavioral, and learning style) to do so. Once they do develop those skills, however, we must move them along. If we do not, we run the risk of doing them a serious disservice and creating a dangerous situation whereby we actually work *against* normalization, rather than towards it.

Section Two: Basic ABA Ideas, to be Adapted to Guide Thinking at Each Level of Programming

Excerpts and Expansions from the Room to Grow Training Manual, Second Edition

(Note: the Room to Grow Training Manual was produced with the assistance of the CUNY Consortium for Developmental Disabilities and the Kennedy Foundation. It was designed to be used as part of a Personalized System of Instruction to help new staff learn concepts within ABA. It was originally written in outline form, a guide for a course instructor. While most of the information was in a convenient outline form, some narrative was provided to go into greater detail when necessary. That strategy has been maintained here, although more explanatory paragraphs have been provided and the organization has been changed a bit for current purposes).

Chapter Four: On the Necessity of Treatment Plans

The behavioral problems that characterize the autistic-spectrum disorders require specific, highly detailed behavior treatment plans. These plans must be carried out by every person in the individual's environment (parents, residential-habilitation specialists, teachers, paraprofessionals, etc.). The failure of any individual to be consistent leads to quite demonstrable differences in student behavior across situations. It is not unusual to see a student who does not tantrum in his mother's presence, but does so with his residential habilitation specialist (or vice versa). Students quickly learn "what flies with whom" and behavior adjusts accordingly.

Treatment plans are constructed after a detailed assessment of the student's behavior. This takes place during a period we call the "baseline," and allows us to target specific skill deficits and/or behavioral excesses. These treatment plans and their accompanying data forms allow us to closely monitor student progress with regard to increasing skills and reducing competing behavior. These treatment plans and the accompanying record keeping devices (see chapter on measuring and charting progress) allow us to ensure that we are not engaging in ineffective or counterproductive treatment plans.

Without behavior treatment plans, behavioral progress would be fairly random. The student would learn isolated skills that were taught to him by one individual or another, but no consistent learning would emerge and the student would likely lose the skills when the teaching was no longer practiced due to the failure of systematic follow-up. This leads to that very sad lament, "he used to be able to do that." Without systematic plans and record keeping, the teacher might try the same strategy for months, unaware that it was not working and thus wasting valuable instructional time.

When working with less severely disabled individuals, such detailed planning and record keeping is superfluous. Gains are generally made more rapidly, and the need for such a fine-grained analysis of progress is not as pronounced. The less disabled individual also picks up skills by imitating behaviors observed in the environment much more easily, again making such intensive teaching unnecessary (referred to in teaching circles as "the machine-gunning of butterflies").

Few are prepared to undertake programming for the autistic. When one first sees an individual with autism, the first reaction might be "where do I begin?" The idea that "they need everything, so teach anything" is demonstrably false and likely to be disastrous. People trained in this discipline are familiar with the "building blocks" of skills, knowing what must be taught first before other skills can be developed. They also know how to break down complex behavior into requisite skills ("task analyses") and to construct precise and reachable goals. As these goals are reached, they build into more complex skills as seen previously.

Because of the need for such systematic plans, communication among team members is crucial. Program books need to be established where plans and data forms are kept. Meetings of the entire team should be held at regular intervals, and the team leader is responsible to ensure that all plans are being carried out correctly and that all programs are current and skills are acquired at an appropriate rate.

Chapter Five: Conceptualizing Behavior

1.   The three-term contingency: in technical language, these three terms are Antecedent, Behavior, and Consequence (the ABCs of behavior).

2.   Antecedent: the stimulus before the behavior occurs that signals that the behavior will be reinforced (Discriminative Stimulus, pronounced "S Dee"), or will not be reinforced (S-Delta).

3.   Dead person's test: anything that a dead person cannot do is behavior. Behavior = response = any bodily movement through space.

4.   Operational definition: a definition that merely describes what happens.

5.   Consequences: reinforcers and punishers.
    A.   A punisher is any stimulus that follows a behavior and makes that behavior less probable in the future. Behavior, and not a person, is reinforced or punished.

    B.   A reinforcer is any stimulus that follows a behavior and makes that behavior more probable in the future.

6.   Types of reinforcers:
    A.   Primary reinforcers are consequences that make us more likely to engage in that same behavior in the future, and we don't need to learn to appreciate these reinforcers (i.e., they are in-born).

    B.   Secondary reinforcers (also called "conditioned reinforcers") are those reinforcers that we have learned to appreciate because they have been paired with primary reinforcement in the past.

    C.   Generalized reinforcers are secondary reinforcers that can be "traded in" for a variety of primary reinforcers. This often takes the form of a "token economy" with points being earned that can be traded in for items from a "menu" (see "how to set up a token economy" below).

D.   "Premack" reinforcers call for you to simply observe the person. You then construct a list (the "Premack hierarchy") of how much time the individual spends engaging in particular activities, with the activities that are engaged in most often highest on the list and the activities that are engaged in least often lowest on the list. The central point of the Premack reinforcer is that you can use activities that are higher on the list as reinforcers for activities that are lower on the list.

7.   Positive vs. Negative Consequences: Positive and negative are defined in terms of how they work, and are <u>not</u> value judgments.
A.   Positive, when talking about either reinforcers or punishers, means that something has been <u>presented</u>.

B.   Negative, when talking about either reinforcers or punishers, means that something has been <u>taken away</u>.

8.   The Contingency: an "if-then" relationship. <u>If</u> my student completes this particular part of his teaching program, <u>then</u> I will give the reinforcer.

9.   Target behavior: the behavior that we are making the focus of analysis or teaching.

10.   Determining individual reinforcers: what is a reinforcer for one individual might be a punisher for another. Do you like (find it reinforcing, to be more precise) to be tickled? How about rap music? Opera? Spicy food? Reinforcers and punishers are individually determined. Construct a Premack hierarchy of what behavior your student is most likely to engage in. Check the activities at the top of the list. You'll find the reinforcers there. Check the bottom, or that behavior that is so unlikely that it doesn't even make the list. Those will be less reinforcing or possibly even punishing.

11.   Extinction: when a behavior is no longer reinforced, the behavior will no longer be performed by the individual.

12.   Extinction burst: before a behavior extinguishes, it increases in frequency, intensity, and variability.

13.   Satiation: the reinforcer is no longer effective because the individual has grown tired of it.

14.   Deprivation: making a reinforcer more potent by not giving it to the individual for a time.

15.   Avoidance: the tendency of individuals to engage in behavior that has previously allowed them to stay away from undesired locations or activities.

16.   Aspects of behavior analytic thinking:
   A.   Determinism: all behavior occurs for a reason. Behavior is governed by laws that are discoverable and useful in changing behavior.

   B.   Single-subject: behavior analysis is based upon individual data. Each student is taken to be a new case, and is compared to his/her own past performance rather than that of another individual.

   C.   Constant graphing and feedback: data are constantly graphed; the subject matter is socially significant, rather than statistically significant, behavior change. This change should be easily visible on a linear, time-series graph.

   D.   Emphasis on reinforcers rather than punishers: Behavior analysis suggests the use of reinforcers instead of punishers.   Punishers lead to avoidance, counter-aggression, and failure to learn what to do instead of merely what not to do. The behavior of the person doing the punishing is also negatively reinforced by removing the undesired behavior, thereby making the behavior of punishing more probable on the part of the trainer. The person delivering the punisher will also be considered a punisher by the student.

   E.   Observable behavior is the subject matter: the focus must be on behavior that can be seen and will be relevant to behavioral goals. Focusing on anything else, such as plans that are too vague to allow you to constantly measure progress, can be distracting.

   F.   Focus on here-and-now: the focus must be on the variables currently maintaining behavior, and not on things that happened in the distant past.

G.   Emphasis on learning theory: the principles of behavior analysis are based upon the laws of operant conditioning, classical conditioning, modeling, and verbal instructions ("rule-governed behavior").

H.   Specific criteria for behavior to be performed, how much, and under what circumstances, are always set beforehand.

I.   Internal and global states (e.g., "he's lazy") are frowned upon as explanations for behavior. Rather, a search is made for environmental factors controlling behavior. If a student is not making progress, look to the teaching program rather than the student for the reason.

J.   Behavior analysis is not manipulative. All techniques are above-board and discussed with students and/or their guardians.

K.   Behavior analysis does not lead to behavior not being done for its own sake.

L.   The job of a behavior analyst is to try to make him/herself unnecessary. The aim for the student is complete independence.

M.   The end-products of the science of behavior analysis are functional analyses: statements of the relationship between environmental variables and behavior.

17.   Thomas Huxley called science "organized common sense." Behavior analysis is common sense directed towards behavior.

18.   Use your own common sense, and remember that sometimes a little knowledge can be a dangerous thing. You wouldn't use your knowledge of a particular medicine to attempt to play the role of a doctor. Until fully trained, don't use your knowledge of behavior to play the role of a qualified behavior analyst.

The Functional Analysis of Behavior

(see also the functional analysis presentation in the appendix)

The functional analysis is the most crucial concept in behavior management. We must therefore cover the topic is some detail. Failure to engage in a good functional analysis will almost always lead to faulty or ineffective behavior treatment plans.

To many people, psychology as a discipline can be summed up in the single question: "why did he do that?" One way to answer this question is to conduct what is known as a functional analysis.

A functional analysis is an experiment. One observes a behavior and forms a hypothesis regarding what "function" the behavior serves. Suppose you see an individual with autism flapping his arms furiously. What function could this behavior serve? There are several possibilities:

1.   The flapping could be an example of perseverative behavior, serving no purpose other than sensory feedback ("it feels good"). We can call this the sensory hypothesis.

2.   The flapping could serve to draw attention to the individual. A nonverbal individual may have no other means of alerting others in the environment of a need (e.g., hunger, thirst, toileting needs). We can call this the communication/attention-seeking hypothesis.

3.   The flapping could serve to intimidate others. The individual with autism may engage in such behavior because it leads to lessened demands (i.e., negative reinforcement in the form of request withdrawal). We can call this the avoidance hypothesis.

4.   The physical exhaustion of the activity could lead to a release of beta-endorphins, a natural painkiller released by the brain in time of physical stress. Beta-endorphins are opiate-like and may lead to euphoria. We can call this the beta-endorphin hypothesis.

How can one decide which of these, or possibly other, theories is the correct one? It is a purely empirical matter. Conduct an A→B-→C analysis and determine which hypothesis is supported by your observations. Then you must test your hypothesis. Each of these conceptions suggests a treatment. If the treatment is successful, one can conclude that a successful and valid functional analysis has been conducted. Let us take the example of the avoidance hypothesis.

During a baseline observation period, we might observe flapping in any number of contexts. As this is a baseline, one might just observe and not attend to the flapping. One would record what percentage of time is spent flapping (perhaps through Partial Interval Recording, see Measuring and Charting Progress).

Your hypothesis is that the flapping serves an avoidance function for this individual. Therefore, during a treatment phase, you would deliberately not remove your presence or requests whenever you observe flapping. Rather, you would stay with the individual and "work through" this behavior. After a brief extinction burst, the flapping should decrease if indeed the behavior is avoidance-based and you carry out the extinction plan properly. Just to make sure that you have confirmed your hypothesis, you might systematically go back to baseline and then back to treatment (a "reversal"). If the flapping is more likely during baseline (allowing the individual to avoid) versus during treatment (working through), then your hypothesis that the flapping serves an avoidance function is confirmed. Your job is now to teach the individual a more socially appropriate way to make needs known.

When conducting your baseline, look for clues regarding what might be maintaining the behavior. It is during the baseline that you draft your hypotheses. If you notice more flapping when you are attending to other individuals and not the student in question, that is a suggestion that the behavior is attention-seeking. If you notice more flapping when you are trying to interact with the student, and the flapping decreases when you stop interaction, that is support for the idea that it is an avoidance behavior.

How to Set up a Token Economy System

Setting up a token economy system is actually a great deal easier than many people suppose it to be. Briefly stated, token economies are a system of exchange whereby particular behavior earns tokens, and these tokens are then traded for other commodities. Token economies are particularly valuable as they are quite normalizing (we all get our paychecks that we trade in for other commodities) and stretch out the supply of other reinforcers (e.g., you may have to earn five tokens to trade it in for a primary). It is unlikely that a student will ever satiate using a generalized reinforcer system. There should always be something new to buy, always something new to get. Further, it is generally not necessary to employ deprivation procedures. Who do you know who thinks they have enough money? No matter how much you have, more is always nice. Contrast this with primary reinforcers such as food. With primaries, deprivation and satiation are serious issues.

To begin using the system, choose the commodity you are going to use. Poker chips, coins, stickers, decorated pieces of laminated cardboard, and points on a point board are common choices.

Once you have your commodity established, sit down with your student. Have a collection of the primary reinforcers (s)he has been earning ready to be used. Begin by simply giving the student the token noncontingently and immediately asking for it back and providing the primary reinforcer. Do this several times. Look for signs that the student is giving you the token without prompting and you know you are ready for the next step.

As you see that the student is now giving you the token back and anticipating the exchange, introduce a contingency. Ask the student to do something *you are certain (s)he can do easily*. Reinforce the performance of this behavior with the presentation of a token and immediately request it back to make the exchange just as you had when you were providing tokens noncontingently. This is your first contingently awarded token. Do this several times to establish the new system.

Of course, you really haven't gained anything yet. The student is still getting a primary reinforcer on every trial. Watch what you can do now, however. Ask the student to perform a skill you are certain (s)he can do, just as before. Award the token. When the student begins to trade in the token, however, quickly ask the student to perform the skill again. When the student does, award another token. Now the student will trade in *both tokens* for the primary. You are now on your way and can begin gradually building the student up to earning several tokens and trading them in. Make sure not to build up requirements too quickly or the behavior may extinguish. Gradually look for more and more accurate responses and longer intervals before trade-in. Keep the system potent, however, and build up patiently. Eventually, you will be able to have different systems working simultaneously (e.g., these pennies are for trading in for primaries for accurate responding during trials, while he also earns points on a board according to a D.R.O. system aimed at reducing perseverative behavior. He'll trade in those points for a trip to the park at the end of the session, or the week, or whatever is appropriate for the student's functioning level).

Example 1

The Three Term-Contingency

$$S^D \text{ --->} \qquad R \text{ --->} \qquad S^{R+}$$

Antecedent   Behavior   Consequence
Model speech   Student imitates   Token & Verbal
Praise

Example 1: A typical three-term contingency applied to a verbal imitation task.

Example 2

Antecedent	Behavior	Consequence
Request made	Student Tantrum	Request Withdrawn

Example 2: A request is made of a student. He begins to tantrum. The teacher then removes the request, not wishing to upset the student. His tantrum is negatively reinforced, and therefore made more likely, by the removal of the request. This is to illustrate a common treatment mistake, not as a suggestion for professional behavior.

Consequence Stimulus

Probability of Behavior	Increase	Presented	Withdrawn
		Positive Reinforcer	Negative Reinforcer
Probability of Behavior	Decrease	Positive Punisher	Negative Punisher

Chapter Six: Writing Behavioral Goals

1.   A behavioral goal is a description of what behavior your student must perform during a particular stage of his program. It must include the following:

  A.   A description of the behavior to be performed.

  B.   The amount of behavior that must be performed.

  C.   When/where the behavior will be performed.

Example: "Gerry will run three laps at the track on Friday afternoon."

Note the components: the behavior is specified (running), how much of the behavior (three laps) is specified, and when and where the behavior will occur (the track on Friday afternoon) is specified. A useful adjunct is to also specify the reinforcer that will follow completion of the goal.

2.   A behavioral goal must be written in concrete terms. The best way to know if you're being concrete is to figure out whether or not the description actually calls for the body to move through space, or some noticeable effect be made on the environment.

 "Will unload the dishwasher after it finishes running" is one part of a behavioral goal. "Will try to think of something to do" is not.

3.   You can tell if a goal is well-written if someone who is watching your student could figure out what the behavioral goal is.

4.   You may have any number of behavioral goals running concurrently (one for each skill that is part of the program).

5.   Appropriate goals have the following characteristics:

  A.   Before teaching, your student can't achieve the goal.

  B.   Completing the goal will be useful to his/her overall behavioral aims.

  C.   It is the next logical step in his/her program. It is a requisite skill to developing more elaborate or useful skills.

D.   With sustainable effort, the goal is achievable (i.e., realistic).

E.   If a behavioral goal will ameliorate a dangerous situation (e.g., self-abuse, darting into traffic, etc.), this goal should take priority over less serious goals.

6.   A baseline measure should be taken to assess current functioning levels to determine what your student is currently capable of and what the next goals should be.

Possible Behavior Goal Sequence for Vocal Imitation

1.   Ann will sit down within two seconds of hearing the cue, "Ann, sit down."

2.   Ann will establish and maintain eye contact for one second after hearing the cue, "Look at me."

3.   Ann will make a random vocal sound after hearing the cue, "say sound."

4.   Ann will approximate the modeled sound after hearing the cue, "say sound" (note that there might be several successive approximations reinforced over time, see chapter on shaping).

5.   Ann will match the modeled sound after hearing the cue, "say sound."

Chapter Seven: Shaping and Chaining

1.   Shaping: the process of building new behavior by differentially reinforcing successive approximations to a desired behavior (the target response).

2.   A behavior that only vaguely resembles the target response can be gradually shaped into the target response via shaping.

3.   To successfully shape behavior, one must:
   A.   Begin by reinforcing a crude approximation to the response.

   B.   After a time, put that crude approximation on extinction (i.e., do not reinforce the crude approximation again).

   C.   An extinction burst will set in, which will lead to a greater frequency and magnitude of behavior, as well as variability in execution.

   D.   As a result of the variability seen with the extinction burst, a closer approximation to the overall goal may be performed.

   E.   Reinforce this closer approximation.

   F.   Repeat steps A-E until the full target response is emitted perfectly.

4.   Be sure never to reinforce an approximation that is physically dangerous (e.g., crossing streets against the lights).

5.   A response class is all behavior that will lead to the same end (e.g., asking for help, which can take the form of raising hands or calling a name or just saying "help"). Not all members of the response class will be equally effective, socially acceptable, or safe.

6.   A behavior chain is a series of responses that must be performed in order to complete a multi-step behavior.

7. The behavior chain can be taught in one of three ways:

    A. Forward chaining: the behavior is taught from the first step to the last step. One does not move on to the next step until the previous one has been mastered.

    B. Backward chaining: all steps in the behavior chain are performed for the student, then all steps but the last one and the student works on this last step. When this last step is mastered, all steps in the behavior chain are performed for the student up to the next-to-last one and the student must perform this next-to-last AND the last step, etc. Eventually, working backward, the student is responsible for performing the entire behavior chain.

    C. Total task presentation: after working with the student on the target step for that day, the student is led through the rest of the chain.

Which of the techniques you will use is dependent upon effectiveness and safety concerns. Our preference is to work using backward chaining whenever not contraindicated by safety concerns. I prefer this because the student sees the finished product as soon as (s)he begins work. If one starts a shoe-tying program with a forward chain, the finished product may not be seen for some time and the student may have no idea what is being worked on. With backward chaining, the finished product is seen immediately.

8. Each step in a behavior chain becomes an S^D for the step to follow. Completing a step becomes a conditioned reinforcer, as it brings the individual closer to completing the overall behavior chain and earning the "terminal" reinforcer (either being finished or some reinforcer given by the teacher).

9. To teach a behavior chain, one constructs a task analysis.

10. A task analysis is a break-down of each individual response in the behavior chain.

11. The individual responses in the behavior chain may need to be shaped.

12.   Task analyses may need to be rewritten for different individuals. A step that might be easily mastered by one individual may need to be broken down further for another individual.

13.   If a student is having difficulty; that is, is stuck on a particular step of a task analysis for a prolonged period of time, that step may need to be broken down further.

14.   Assume nothing when you construct a task analysis. Put down every single step that the student must perform.

15.   If unsure about the construction of a task analysis, go through the behavior chain yourself, writing down every bodily movement.

16.   Different types of cues may be provided to teach each step in the task analysis:
   A.   Verbal cues are spoken directions or descriptions of behavior.

   B.   Visual cues may be models of the behavior to be imitated, or some other visual representation of the step.

   C.   Physical cues involve actual physical contact (e.g., a hand-over-hand technique that allows the teacher to mold behavior into the proper form).

17.   Extra prompts should be faded out (eliminated) as soon as possible to avoid the student becoming dependent on them. This fading should be gradual (e.g., by speaking gradually more and more softly, saying less and less of the word, holding the hand progressively more and more lightly, etc.).

18.   Be careful not to prompt more than necessary.

19.   When delivering a verbal cue, it is best to say it once and then give a physical prompt if needed. This will teach the student to respond after the first verbal cue. Giving an excessive number of verbal cues will teach the student that you do not expect performance after the first cue. Reinforce responses that are performed independently or after one verbal cue when they are within the student's repertoire. Do not reinforce excessively prompted responses.

The Extinction Burst

Few concepts in behavior analysis are as crucial as the extinction burst. As stated above, when one ceases to reinforce a previously reinforced behavior, this is called an extinction procedure. It is very commonly accompanied by what is known as an extinction burst. During the burst, the behavior will temporarily get worse before it gets better. The behavior will increase in frequency, magnitude, and variability. We place it here because of its role in shaping new behavior, but please review this section when reading about extinction procedures in subsequent chapters.

The untrained in behavior analysis often read somewhere about extinction procedures, but not the extinction burst. When they institute an extinction procedure for a behavior, e.g. self-abuse, they are unaware that it will likely get worse before getting better.

Let us suppose that a student is hitting herself in the head with her open hand. An extinction procedure is instituted:

1.   No one pays attention when she hits herself.

2.   They do pay attention when she's not engaging in the behavior (never do an extinction plan alone, always reinforce some other behavior at the same time).

The student displays the behavior we would call the extinction burst. She stops hitting herself with her hand, and starts hitting herself with a closed fist. The teacher, unaware of the temporary nature of the extinction burst, calls off the extinction procedure, fearing it is being counter-productive.

Unfortunately, through the poor use of behavioral technique, this teacher has made the behavior much worse. Is the student likely to go back to hitting her head with her open hand? No, that didn't work to get attention. Using her fist was what worked. Which do you think she'll do from now on? Right, use the fist. If the extinction burst had been weathered, if the student would have hit her head with the fist and no one had attended, the student would have stopped and would probably not be engaging in ANY self-abuse (possibly after trying a few more variations first).

This is where we must remember the old axiom that a little knowledge can be a dangerous thing. One must know about the extinction burst and plan for it. We have not written extinction plans for students when we determined during baseline that the behavior could become too severe to ignore. If the extinction burst cannot be weathered, if injury to the student or others is likely, then an extinction plan SHOULD NOT BE BEGUN. USE ANOTHER BEHAVIOR MANAGEMENT STRATEGY.

As a final note, just as with reinforcers and punishers, one extinguishes a BEHAVIOR, not a person. I can ignore the fact that you are hitting yourself and continue working with you. I ignore the behavior, not the individual.

Sample Task Analysis: Putting on a Shirt

S<u>D</u>	Behavior	Consequence
1. "Pick it up"	Student picks up shirt	"Very good" & student has shirt.
2. Student is holding shirt "Put it on"	Student pulls shirt over head	"Very good" & shirt is over head
3. Shirt is over-head & "Pull your head through"	Student pokes head through collar	"You did it" & head is through collar
4. Head is through collar & "Put your left arm through the sleeve"	Student puts left arm through sleeve	"Way to go!" & arm is through sleeve
5. Arm is through sleeve & "Now the other arm through"	Student puts right arm through sleeve	"Yeah!" & Both arms are in
6. Shirt is on & "Tuck it in"	Student tucks shirt in	"ALL DONE" & Shirt is on.

Chapter Eight: Measuring and Charting Progress

1.   Virtually all behavior analytic interventions use a line or bar graph or standard celeration chart or some other visual representation of the data under consideration. These graphs allow for the immediate assessment of progress, and avoid difficulties related to not being able to judge whether or not a student is making progress.

2.   Along the horizontal axis is generally some unit of time, and along the vertical axis is usually some behavioral measure that explains what is being looked at (e.g., percentage of time intervals where a particular behavior was seen, number of times a behavior occurs, etc.).

3.   Types of behavioral measures include:

A.   Frequency: how many times did the behavior occur? The central question here is quantity of responses, even if it is just whether or not the behavior occurred at all (presence or absence of response). This is most easily done with two observers or with relatively low frequency responses. If one person does frequency recording with high-rate responses, one is doing nothing but counting (no teaching is taking place).

B.   Duration: for how long does the behavior take place? This is appropriate for responses that may take a long time to complete (e.g., avoidance screaming during an extinction burst).

C.   Magnitude: some qualitative description of the scope of behavior (e.g., the number of pounds lifted, or the heart rate achieved and sustained if one were working on an exercise program). This is best used for responses where the sheer number of times it occurs is not as important as how intense the behavior was (e.g., exercise for heart rate).

D.   Latency: how long after a cue was given did it take for the behavior to occur? This is best when the issue is how quickly an individual responds to a prompt.

E.   Rate: number of responses per some unit of time. This is best for responses where the issue is how many times the individual engages in a particular response in a given period of time (e.g., inappropriate calling out during a group lesson).

F.   Topography: a description of the form of behavior exhibited. This is best when one desires a description of the behavior (e.g., the manner in which a student hits himself, which may be important for assessing injury potential or the presence of an extinction burst).

4.   Data sheets exist commercially to collect such data, or new data sheets can be designed. Precise data should be collected any time a behavior is under consideration for a treatment plan.

5.   Data can be collected in a number of ways, depending upon what is easiest in the situation:

A.   Continuous data recording: best if used with low frequency responses, this is watching and rating behavior with no breaks.

B.   Momentary time sampling: good for high frequency responses when one is alone. Momentary time sampling calls for the observer to look for the presence or absence of a particular behavior for one second every interval (e.g., at the end of every minute, the observer looks to see if the student is engaging in a particular response *at that second*). One would mark "yes" if the behavior was occurring at the moment one looked up, and "no" if the behavior was not occurring at the moment (s)he looked up. This may tend to under-estimate how frequently the behavior occurs.

C.   Partial interval recording: also good for high frequency responses, partial interval recording calls for the observer to note whether or not a particular behavior occurred during a particular interval. One would simply mark "yes" if the behavior did occur *at least once* during the interval or "no" if the behavior did not occur during the interval. Note that with both momentary time sampling and partial interval recording, one may not get a true picture of the behavior. How many times the behavior occurs is not recorded. One is only left with a percentage of intervals during which the behavior was observed.

D.   Anecdotal recording: a narrative of what transpired. This is best if one is only observing and not trying to teach. Keep descriptions to what can be observed by two people (i.e., do not hypothesize as to causes, simply describe action as though you were a video camera).

Chapter Nine: Common Techniques

1. Positive reinforcement: the cornerstone of behavior analysis. Used to increase target responses in most teaching situations, it also serves a feedback function in that it allows the student to know when responses are being performed correctly. A positive reinforcer is any stimulus that, when delivered after a behavior, tends to make that behavior more probable in the future.

2. Negative reinforcement: very often at the root of avoidance behavior. Negative reinforcement is observed when a behavior becomes more probable when a stimulus is withdrawn whenever that response is performed (e.g., tantrums that become more frequent because it leads to a withdrawal of demands).

3. Extinction: used to eliminate undesired behavior by not reinforcing it. Be wary of the extinction burst (see shaping and chaining chapter). While doing an extinction procedure, always reinforce some other response. This will add to the effectiveness of your extinction plan by giving the individual an alternate means of obtaining reinforcement.

4. DRO (Differential Reinforcement of Other behavior, also called Omission Training and DRZ: Differential Reinforcement of Zero Rates): a behavior-reduction technique that is based upon both time AND responses. With a DRO procedure, you get the reinforcer as long as you have NOT engaged in some specified behavior for the specified time period. A DRO procedure might be used to eliminate an undesirable behavior such as smoking or perseverative flapping. After figuring out roughly how frequently a student smokes cigarettes (or flaps, or hits self, or any other undesired behavior), pre-set an interval lower than this baseline time. When you begin the procedure, you would deliver a reinforcer for every pre-specified time period that passes that (s)he does NOT engage in the behavior. By gradually increasing the length of time that your student must go without engaging in the response, you'll soon find him/her not engaging in the response at all.

5. DRH (Differential Reinforcement of High rates of behavior): the reinforcer is only delivered if a certain minimum number of responses have been emitted in a given time period (e.g., a minimum number of minutes must be spent bicycling within a

given week, or a certain minimum number of math examples must be accurately completed within ten minutes before one is eligible to receive reinforcement).

6. DRI (Differential Reinforcement of Incompatible behavior): the behavior that you wish to eliminate is placed on extinction, while a behavior that cannot physically be performed at the same time as the behavior that you wish to eliminate is reinforced (e.g., rather than address hand-flapping while walking, you simply reinforce appropriate "hands in pockets" while walking: hand-flapping and hands in pockets are physically incompatible).

7. Intermittent reinforcement: not giving a reinforcer every time the behavior occurs, but only after a certain number of responses have been emitted, or reinforcing the first response after a given time period has elapsed (see special section at the end of the chapter).

8. Response cost: the key to a "response cost" procedure is that you "pay for your mistakes." With a response cost procedure, engaging in some undesirable behavior leads to the loss of some desired commodity or privilege. The key to a response cost procedure is that you make the loss noticeable, but not so dramatic that you can no longer earn the desired end (and therefore just stop trying). In a token economy, one might use a response cost procedure whereby an undesired behavior (e.g., verbal cursing) might lead to a loss of previously earned reinforcers.

9. Time-out: the student is removed from on-going reinforcement for a short period of time contingent upon the emission of inappropriate behavior. Time-out can be exclusionary (removing the individual from the setting after the inappropriate behavior occurs) or inclusionary (the individual is not removed, but a conditioned reinforcer, such as a ribbon that signals eligibility to participate in a reinforcing activity, is removed for a matter of minutes after the inappropriate behavior occurs). Inclusionary time-out is often easier to manage and more humane than exclusionary time-out. When using either type of time-out, keep it brief and make sure that the individual is not misbehaving when the time-out period is up. DO NOT terminate a time-out when the individual is misbehaving or you will be reinforcing that misbehavior. As mentioned earlier (see sections on functional analysis) NEVER use time-out for avoidance behavior or you will

merely be reinforcing the inappropriate behavior.

10.   Satiation: you noncontingently deliver the reinforcer that has been maintaining misbehavior. If a student is stealing food, for example, you might give a very large amount of food before the opportunity to steal has presented itself.

11.   Negative practice: if a student has engaged in some undesired behavior, (s)he is made to do it again and again. This may be highly confusing, however, and is often not recommended.

12.   Overcorrection: the essence of an overcorrection procedure is to undo the damage your behavior has caused, plus interest. If one deliberately spills a drink, rather than merely cleaning the spill one would clean the whole table and possibly the surrounding area. The misbehavior becomes "too much trouble" to perform.

13.   Behavior analysts subscribe to something called the "Least Restrictive Treatment model." See special section, below.

14.   Your overriding goal should always be to increase desired behavior. Reducing undesired behavior should be secondary. REINFORCEMENT-BASED PROCEDURES ARE ALWAYS PREFERRED.

Intermittent Reinforcement

The importance of intermittent reinforcement cannot be overstated. Intermittent reinforcement leads to behavior that is more resistant to extinction (e.g., you continue to put money into a slot machine even if it doesn't pay off, but stop very quickly when a soda machine does not give you the soda you expect after putting your money in). This is important when teaching a new skill, as one would not want this skill to extinguish. After a time, move from continuous to intermittent reinforcement in order to guard against extinction.

Knowledge of intermittent reinforcement is also crucial when considering behavior that one wishes to eliminate. If one gives in to screaming and allows the student to avoid even every once in a while, that is intermittent reinforcement (just like the slot machine). The student never knows when screaming will "pay off" and tends to engage in the behavior for a much longer time than if the behavior had been continuously reinforced and then extinguished. How is the student even supposed to realize that the behavior is on extinction if it has been on intermittent reinforcement? Maybe this is just one of those times when you're holding out, and maybe you'll eventually give in and reinforce the screaming just like those other times. He may as well keep at it.

When teaching a desired behavior, one should try to change over from continuous to intermittent reinforcement as soon as possible. One can base intermittency on time (interval) or the number of responses (ratio). Requirements can be the same each time (fixed) or change (variable). Variable Ratio schedules tend to lead to very high, steady rates of behavior (as in the slot machine example). As stated above, this will lead to behavior that is resistant to extinction and this is also more normalizing. Most of us work on an intermittent reinforcement schedule; not everything we do always works out as we want. Intermittent reinforcement can also lead to a build-up of what we would call frustration tolerance.

The Least Restrictive Treatment Model

As stated above, behavior analysts subscribe to something called the Least Restrictive Treatment Model. What this basically means is that all treatment techniques that are less intrusive (or aversive) must be experimentally documented as ineffective before one moves on to a more intrusive (or aversive) procedure. This is an ethical stance, and a practical one as well. More aversive techniques will lead to the individual seeking to avoid the teacher, and possibly counter-aggressing.

Note that the less intrusive procedure must be EXPERIMENTALLY PROVEN to be ineffective before one moves on and attempts a more intrusive procedure. That means painstaking treatment plan execution and data collection before one can move on to a more intrusive procedure. If one attempts a more intrusive procedure before experimentally demonstrating that a less intrusive procedure is ineffective, one is violating the accepted ethical practice of behavior analysis. Most agencies will have their own guidelines on the use of intrusive procedures, but it is also widely accepted that aversives should not be used except under the most tightly supervised conditions, and only then after approval has been obtained from guardians, agency, and state governing bodies.

Chapter Ten: Effective Self-Management

1.   Every behavior leads to some kind of consequence. Certain
      factors figure into every decision:
      A.   What sort of reinforcer or punisher will come (how
            potent)?

      B.   How much of it will we receive (magnitude)?

      C.   How long will it take to get that reinforcer or punisher
            (delay)?

      D.   In general, we seek out potent reinforcers, ones that we
            will receive in large magnitudes, and with the least amount
            of delay. We also tend to put off punishing behavior for as
            long as possible.

2.   Self-monitoring: to observe and accurately judge one's own
      behavior.

3.   Self-reinforcement: to deliver consequences appropriately after
      one's own behavior, only when they are called for by the
      treatment plan.

4.   Self-management: systematically applying behavior analysis to
      one's own actions so as to bring about desired behavior.

5.   Some techniques for bringing about desired behavior change
      work from the antecedent side of the three-term contingency
      (e.g., removing cues for inappropriate behavior, providing cues
      for appropriate behavior, making sure you come into contact
      with natural cues for appropriate behavior, setting aside some
      particular time or place to engage in some appropriate behavior).

6.   Another strategy for self-management is to use self-monitoring.
      Self-monitoring alone has been shown to improve behavior from
      smoking to exercise to conversation, a phenomenon known as
      "reactivity."

7.   You must self-monitor before you know if a behavior that you
      can self-reinforce has occurred.

8.   In general, the more delayed the consequence, the weaker the effect on behavior.

9.   Adding other consequences, immediate and powerful ones, may promote behavior change.   This is what we call "self-reinforcement."

10.   This effect can be increased by making our goals public. In addition to private scrutiny, we also add social pressure to keep us complying with our goals.

11.   A reinforcer should be chosen that you will have only for completing a behavioral goal, and does not come for any other reason.

12.   Satiation, the losing of a reinforcer's effectiveness, can occur if the reinforcer comes too frequently (i.e., without sufficient "deprivation").

13.   Using a reinforcer that you can get in other ways besides completing the target behavior tears down the link between completing a behavior goal and obtaining the reinforcer. This will undermine the effectiveness of the reinforcer, and your training program.

14.   The reinforcer should be able to be taken fairly soon after the behavior occurs. The more delayed the reinforcer, the less effective it will be.

15.   The whole reason for this reinforcer is to equalize out the discrepancy between long and short-term consequences. Consider exercising. We pit the short-term consequence (e.g., feeling exhaustion) against the long-term consequences (e.g., a more fit body). Reinforcers help to keep us on track.

16.   Make sure that your consequence really is a reinforcer. Not every consequence is a reinforcer.

17.   Learning self-management skills may be your student's most useful skill on the road to more normal behavior. You can remind your student that:
      A.   Not every instance of your behavior can be watched by somebody else.

B.   Self-management skills will help you to continue to behave appropriately long after any intensive teaching effort has ended.

C.   Your appropriate behavior may also generalize, or transfer to other settings or activities.

D.   Self-management skills can keep you engaging in a behavior when the natural outcomes are too weak or delayed to maintain behavior.

E.   Some people feel more comfortable using self-management as opposed to being continuously watched by someone else.

F.   Self-management may itself be rewarding. Feeling like you yourself have orchestrated and accomplished your goals may give you the confidence to go on and accomplish even more.

18.   To teach self-management, begin by having the teacher reinforce the desired behavior. Then prompt the student to reinforce his desirable behavior, and gradually fade your prompts. Give reinforcers for accuracy in self-monitoring and self-reinforcement when the student is totally responsible for self-monitoring and self-reinforcing (i.e., when all prompts have been faded).

19.   Update self-management plans frequently.

20.   Cheating is the bane of any self-management program.

21.   Gains are useless unless they are maintained. The student must continue to engage in the self-management plan as a lifestyle, and not just as a temporary adjustment.

22.   Self-management skills training is the best insurance one has that the gains will be maintained by the student after teaching has ended.

Generalization and Maintenance

It has become a truism among behavior analysts that behavioral gains are pointless unless these gains are going to be maintained after intensive teaching has ended. Further, teaching is pointless unless the new behavior is also displayed in other appropriate settings. These are the twin topics of maintenance and generalization.

To ensure maintenance and/or generalization, one must plan and program. Neither, unfortunately, often occurs spontaneously. To plan for maintenance, one must first move from continuous to intermittent reinforcement. One must also plan some means of having the responsibility for reinforcing the appropriate behavior to be taken over by someone else in the environment where the behavior should be displayed. This may mean teaching another individual in the student's setting to deliver reinforcers appropriately, or may call for teaching self-management skills.

To attempt to ensure generalization, one would have to engage in what is known as "loose" teaching. This means varying as many aspects of the teaching situation as possible, once the skill has reached some criteria of mastery using the initial teaching methodology. One would vary such things as:

A.   Time of day that one teaches
B.   The exact verbal instructions
C.   The setting in which one teaches
D.   Who is doing the teaching
E.   What tone of voice is used
F.   The order of task presentation
G.   The gender of the teacher
H.   The physical size of the teacher
I.   The number of other people present
J.   The level of background noise present
K.   The number of other students being taught simultaneously.

As you can see, generalization will be made most probable when one varies as many aspects of the teaching situation as possible. Even changing what one wears when teaching can aid in generalization.

Chapter Eleven:
Contingency Contracting

1.   Contingency contracting turns naggers into helpers, by giving them a specific job.

2.   Given a particular responsibility, people are less inclined to just "nag" randomly.

3.   The contractor will be asked to monitor progress and to judge compliance or non-compliance with goals in keeping with a written contract.   The contractor will therefore judge when consequences should be administered.

4.   A parent or favored staff member is a natural contractor relationship.

5.   If your student prefers someone else, suggest that (s)he:
      A.   Pick a contractor whose approval or knowledge of his/her success would be very reinforcing (a "type one").

      B.   Pick a contractor whose disapproval or knowledge of failure would be very aversive (a "type two").

6.   A friend would be a good example of a type one contractor. An obnoxious rival of some sort serves as a good type two contractor. Most people gravitate toward type one, but there are those who respond better to the latter type of pressure. In keeping with the behavior analytic emphasis on reinforcement instead of aversives, we strongly advise getting a type one contractor.

7.   Regardless of the type of contractor, your student must tell the contractor: "Be tough! This is for my own good, and if I don't do as I should, carry out the consequences that we have set up."

8.   Someone who is too nice or feels sorry for your student, even in the name of "being understanding," will be counter-productive.

9.   When constructing a contract, the idea is to be as business-like as possible:
      A.   The behavior specified in the contract should be easily described in terms of whether it occurred or did not occur.

B.   Both parties entering into the contract must realize that they are undertaking a serious effort that will only be successful if both parties keep to their stated behavior.

10.   Once the behavior of both parties is set, an equally important task is the creation of the monitoring and record keeping system.

11.   An example of where contingency contracting would be useful is in the area of damaging habits: "if less than 3 destructive acts are performed per day during this week, then 5 points towards the reinforcer, _____ will be given. If this goal is not met, a reminder in the form of _____ will be delivered."

12.   Your contingency contract should specify consequences for adherence and violations.

13.   Contingency contracts can be normalizing and make students feel very adult.

14.   Contingency contracts require a functioning level that will allow both student and contractor to do their parts on either end of the contract.

Chapter Twelve: Imitation

1.   Imitation is said to be observed when one individual behaves as another individual has behaved.

2.   Imitation skills may need to be taught as skills unto themselves. Do not assume that an individual will already have imitation skills in his behavioral repertoire.

3.   The person who is performing the action to be copied is known as the model. His/her behavior is sometimes also called a model or a visual cue.

4.   Teaching imitation skills is important in that it can dramatically cut down the time required to teach a skill. If every single behavior that an individual was going to learn needed to be taught via a task analysis, it would take quite a while to develop even rudimentary skills. If a student can imitate, however, rather than a complex task analysis being used to teach each skill, a model can simply say "do this" and teach through imitation.

5.   In the early stages of teaching, approximations to a model's behavior are acceptable and may be reinforced. As time passes, however, these approximations should give way to matches, with the behavior of the model being copied precisely.

6.   A student is said to show "generalized imitation" when (s)he imitates behavior that (s)he has never received reinforcement for imitating or approximating before (i.e., the student now imitates new or "novel" behaviors never seen previously).

7.   Generalized motor and verbal imitation training are two of the building-block skills that are worked on after eye contact and appropriate sitting have been taught.

8.   Ease in acquiring vocal imitation skills is associated with a better prognosis in some students with autism.

9.   When teaching motor imitation, give one verbal cue of "do this" and perform the action. If the student does not match or approximate, use a physical prompt to guide him in performing the action. Give the student an opportunity to imitate the behavior again. If the student does imitate without additional

prompts, make sure to reinforce.

10.   Make sure to use "do this" or "do what I do" as a cue, rather than a description of the behavior such as "touch your nose." The object here is teach the skill of imitating what you do, not necessarily just to locate your nose.

11.   When teaching either verbal or motor imitation, make sure to establish eye contact before presenting a model. A student cannot imitate what he cannot see.

12.   When teaching verbal imitation, use "say ____ " as your model or just model the sound without the "say."

13.   Start by attempting to teach sounds that the student already spontaneously makes. Using this strategy, you will know that the skill is within his ability, and you just need to teach him to make the sound at the appropriate time (i.e., after your cue).

14.   Move on to harder sounds and into actual words as student progress dictates.

15.   Try to introduce functional words into the verbal imitation training as soon as possible.

16.   Try to introduce functional skills into the motor imitation training as soon as possible.

17.   By making what you teach in imitation training actually functional for the student, you increase the probability that these skills will be independently displayed in everyday life. If your student displays functional skills, that will lead to natural reinforcers from the environment.

Chapter Thirteen: Discrete Trial Teaching

We deliberately left this section for last, even after the philosophical admonition that was in the original manual. The reason for this is quite simple. In the popular mind, discrete trial teaching has BECOME applied behavior analysis. People think that discrete trial teaching is all there is to ABA, when in fact it is only one of its myriad techniques. Countless "programmers" roam the countryside and cities, offering discrete trial instruction to families of children with autism. These individuals frequently have very limited knowledge of the information that has preceded this, and their students suffer as a result. We hope no one using this manual will fall into this trap.

1.   Discrete trial teaching is the three term contingency (A → B → C) relationship described above as applied to teaching new skills.

2.   The "A" is the Antecedent that generally takes the form of the instruction provided by the therapist/trainer.

3.   The "B" is the behavior the student must perform.

4.   The "C" is the consequence provided.

5.   There are several "styles" or approaches to doing discrete trial instruction. Two of the most common are Errorless Learning and No-no prompting.

6.   In Errorless learning, the student is not allowed to make a mistake on any given trial. If a person does not perform the behavior correctly, either doing it incorrectly OR doing nothing, (s)he is prompted through it correctly before a new trial begins. If possible, (s)he is prevented from making the incorrect response in the first place through careful prompting.

An example of a motor imitation program in an errorless paradigm:

A: Therapist says "Do this" and claps two times
B: The student claps two times
C: Therapist says "Good doing what I do" and delivers a "high five."

The trial is over, and a new one begins.

Alternate example:

A: Therapist says "Do this" and claps two times
B: The student does not move
C: Therapist takes students hands and physically prompts two claps. While doing this, she says "This is doing what I do."

The trial is over and a new one begins.

7.   In errorless learning, an antecedent marks the beginning of a new trial. One does not repeat verbal cues. The slogan is "one verbal, then one physical prompt."

8.   Another style of doing discrete trial instruction is called "No-no prompting."

9.   In "No-no prompting," trials look exactly the same as errorless learning if the student performs the action correctly after the first cue.

10.   "No-no prompting" differs from errorless learning in error correction. Rather than physically prompting the response after the first failure to respond correctly, the student is led through a three stage process. After the first incorrect response (or no response) the therapist says "no" and turns her head slightly. The antecedent is given again. If the student again does not perform the response correctly, the therapist again says "no" with the head turn. After the third antecedent, if the student does not perform the response correctly (s)he will receive a physical prompt. Note that sometimes teachers substitute "nope" or other "softer" variations for "no."

11.   Prompting verbal responses is more difficult than motor responses.

12.   After a number of trials in which the student does not respond appropriately, sometimes "massed practice" is conducted where the student is led through the drill repeatedly until (s)he begins to demonstrate the skill independently. The student is prompted immediately on every trial. This is not always recommended, as it can be aversive.

13.   Both errorless learning and "no-no prompting" have benefits and drawbacks.   Errorless learning may help students learn to respond to the first request, but may also lead to "prompt dependency," wherein students wait to be prompted through activity.   Fading of prompts must be skillfully done.   "No-no prompting" guards against such prompt dependency but may not foster compliance with first requests.

14.   Which style to use is an empirical question related to student learning style. As in all things behavior analytic, the data guide the decision-making process.

15.   Regardless of prompting strategy, the basic rules of reinforcement described above must be maintained:
       A.   Reinforcers must be individually chosen

       B.   Reinforcers must come immediately after the correct response

       C.   Descriptive praise, in which you say what the individual has done well (e.g., "Nice talking!") is employed

       D.   As skills are learned, reinforcement is delivered intermittently to promote generalization and maintenance.

16.   The response required of the student must be carefully spelled out. For each trial, there should be pre-set criteria for correct responding and subsequent reinforcement. It should not be a "judgment call." In some programs, novel responding may be a goal. In this case, there should still be set and objective criteria for correct responding.

17.   As skills are learned in discrete trial, loose teaching (see above) should be used to foster generalization of responding.

18.   The goal of discrete trial teaching is to improve lagging skills. When the student no longer needs 1 to 1 instruction, efforts should be made to normalize instruction and introduce peer group participation as soon as possible. Students who are only taught by discrete trial rarely generalize their skills to more everyday situations.

19.   The discrete trial teaching situation should not be aversive to the student.   Allowing students to have as much choice of reinforcers and programming as possible will make sessions more productive. Varying the teaching situation (e.g., location, teacher, stimuli) will make teaching more interesting and foster generalization.

20.   Students can use self-management in discrete trial teaching.

Section Three:
A Longitudinal Study

Author's Note: What follows next is a longitudinal study conducted by myself, Sara Birch, and Frederica Blausten. The study traces graduation placements of graduates from the preschool program of AMAC, Inc.

We debated about including the study, as it was conducted before AMAC instituted the graduated model. We finally decided to include it, however, as it shows the power of behavioral techniques in general, and provides empirical data to support the systematic application of behavioral principles.

The Effect of Behavioral Interventions
on the Graduation Placement of Preschool Students
with Autism and other Developmental Disabilities

Since the 1970s, placement in the Least Restrictive Environment (LRE) has been the overriding goal of parents and professionals concerned with the developmentally disabled in general, and students with autism in particular. While many programs promise to help students to achieve LRE placement, many, if not most programs, have failed to show any efficacy in achieving this aim (Clinical Practice Guideline: Report of the Recommendations, Autism and Pervasive Developmental Disorders, New York State Department of Health Early Intervention Program). There are a wide variety of treatment options available, and parents are left with a bewildering array to choose from (e.g., Guralick, 1998).

Over the past several years, there has also been increasing concern with the national expansion of Special Education services. Faced with skyrocketing costs and shrinking budgets, many states are looking for ways to cut the costs associated with Special Education. The State of New York, for example, has charged preschool providers with the task of moving 25% of special education preschool students to less restrictive environments as an all-inclusive standard for their required annual business plans (Memo from New York State Education Department regarding Chapter 474 of the Laws of 1996, 4410 of the Education Law, October, 1996).

This mandate to move students to less restrictive placements is indeed a worthy goal. What it does not specify, however, is a crucial component. How are students to be moved into these less restrictive environments?   One common strategy has been to create self-contained classrooms within general education settings. Limited research has been done, however, as regards the effectiveness of these models for children with autism.

A further problem is that such self-contained settings do not allow for much in the way of opportunities for mainstreaming or interaction with normally developing peers. Therefore, a much more attractive option may be to prepare students to rejoin their peers in actual mainstream classrooms. Achieving this goal would have the multiple benefits of:

1.   Exposing students to far greater opportunities for interaction with typically developing peers and thus far greater opportunities for normalization,

2.   Allowing self-contained Special Education settings to concentrate their resources on those who most need the more intensive assistance,

3.   Realizing the state-mandated goal of successfully placing students into less restrictive mainstream environments.

Recently, a great deal of interest has been shown in programs that teach using the Applied Behavior Analytic (ABA) model, particularly small programs with high staff to student ratios that emphasize Discrete Trial Teaching. Few programs are funded at a level that allows for this intensive level of instruction, however. If such programs are not financially feasible, an alternative must be sought.

The current study is a longitudinal analysis of the graduation placements of students from the preschool of the Association in Manhattan for Autistic Children, Inc. (AMAC). AMAC assumed control over this preschool from a prior agency in 1988, and continued to conduct the preschool in keeping with the previous agency's psychoanalytic orientation. When a new Executive Director assumed control of AMAC in the Summer of 1992, the preschool became behavioral in focus and philosophy. The AMAC preschool maintained the prior staffing structure of seven students to two adults in a classroom. The orientation was changed, however, to a data-based system where student behavior was analyzed in keeping with applied behavior analytic philosophy, and staff behavior changed in keeping with the outcomes of these analyses.

The current analysis focuses on the graduation placements of two years of the psychoanalytic preschool, and the succeeding four years of graduates from AMAC's behavioral preschool. The feasibility of utilizing behavioral methodology as a means of moving students into LRE will be empirically analyzed.

Method

Subjects

The students ranged in age from 2.4 to 4.6 years of age upon admission to the preschool. The students were diagnosed with disorders including Autism, Pervasive Developmental Disorder, and severe emotional disturbance (called Preschoolers with a Disability during the first four years under consideration). All students met criteria for requiring center-based programs, the diagnoses being made through outside agencies. These diagnoses were subsequently confirmed by on-site psychiatrists and psychologists, using DSM-IV criteria. The only students who were not accepted at any time were those whose primary diagnosis was mental retardation, sensory impairment, or traumatic brain injury. No student scored in the normal range of intelligence upon admission to the preschool.

All students lived within the five boroughs of New York City. All ethnic and socio-economic groups were represented, reflecting the diversity of New York City. All students graduated if they reached age 5 by September 1st and thus became eligible for kindergarten in accordance with New York State attendance laws.

Procedure

Student records were analyzed by an independent investigator who was blind as to the purpose of the analysis. The investigator went through student records for the following information:

1.   Student age at admission and upon graduation or transfer,

2.   Diagnosis at admission and upon graduation or transfer (if available),

3.   IQ at admission,

4.   If the student had been in a prior Special Education placement, and

5.   Where the student was placed following graduation.

Graduates of the preschool were grouped into three school-age educational placements that roughly mirror those of Lovaas (1987). Students were placed in one of the following three programs upon graduation. These placements reflect a continuum of options from most to least restrictive environments.

1.   Special education classes for students with autism (self-contained, center-based classes in centralized facilities, in New York City known as SIE-III, Specialized Instructional Environments). This is the most restrictive environment, with comparatively high staff to student ratios. There is no access to mainstream environments, nor to typically developing peers. All children carry the classification of autism.

2.   Special education classes for students with mild delays (housed in neighborhood public schools, in New York City known as MIS-IV, Modified Instructional Setting). These programs have a

student to staff ratio of approximately ten students per one teacher and two teacher assistants. Students have access to inclusion opportunities and may integrate with typically developing peers during such periods as lunch and recess, as well as those academic classes where they can keep pace with their normally developing peers. All children are classified as speech impaired or learning disabled or having mild emotional problems.

3.   Community kindergarten classes. Kindergarten classes are available within each local elementary school. Classes range in size from 18-22 children. Larger classes have teacher assistants, and no students are classified as disabled.

Program Descriptions

When discussing the two models under consideration, several factors remained constant.

1.   The length of the school day remained at 5.5 hours.

2.   Staffing ratios remained at seven students to one teacher and one teacher assistant, supplemented by related services as mandated on student IEPs.

3.   The entire school was organized around the model in question. The classrooms were part of the model existent throughout the entire agency (which included adult services, recreation, summer camp and eventually a school age program).

4.   Levels of related service provision remained constant, in keeping with student IEP mandates.

During the first two years under consideration, students participated in what was called a "therapeutic milieu". The model of the program was psychodynamic in orientation, and therefore activities were arranged in order to encourage expression of unexpressed trauma and emotion.

Students engaged in supervised play during the day, staffing being provided by a Certified Special Education teacher assisted by college level uncertified assistants. In addition to these services, related services were provided on a pull-out model. These related services included speech, occupational therapy and counseling. Common activities included playing with puppets and expression through music or movement.

Teachers were supervised by a psychologist trained within the psychodynamic orientation. Supervision was provided regarding how to spct the signs of emotional trauma, and how to help students to express themselves through play, music and movement.

Following the changeover to a behavioral model, activities shifted in focus to a skill-building model. Staffing levels remained constant, but altered in focus. Rather than playing with puppets or engaging in expressive dance, for example, students were taught functional skills through a task analysis model. Related services became push-in models, and worked in concert with the teachers and teacher assistants on the skill-building programs.

Teachers were supervised by psychologists who met criteria to become Board Certified Behavior Analysts (and in fact the last of these became one when the certification became available). Supervision was provided in data-based decision making and various techniques of group behavior management, as well as individualized instruction concepts (shaping, chaining, prompting and fading, etc.). Other specific changes are detailed within the discussion section.

Results

The composition of the student body did not change significantly during the six years of analysis. The percentage of students initially diagnosed with autism at intake ranged from 42 - 80%.

The outcome data for all students are summarized on Table 1.

As can be seen, of the graduates from the 90-91 school year, 80% were placed into special education classes for the autistic, while 20% of the students were placed into MIS community classes for those with mild delays. These placements exactly mirror student diagnosis at entry, with 80% of the students being diagnosed as autistic prior to entering the preschool, and 80% being diagnosed as autistic following preschool. At 91-92 graduation, 67% of the students were placed into classes for the autistic, with the other 33% being placed into MIS community classes for mildly delayed students. No student originally diagnosed as autistic lost this diagnosis. In neither year did any student achieve mainstream functioning. These results are similar to the results seen with the minimal treatment control group of the Lovaas (1987) study.

Table 1.
Graduation Placements of Students, Broken Down by Year (rounded off)

Year	% SIE classes	% MIS classes	% Community Kindergarten
1990-1991	80%	20%	—
1991-1992	67%	33%	—
1992-1993	45%	49%	6%
1993-1994	38%	56%	6%
1994-1995	29%	56%	15%
1995-1996	36%	59%	5%

Graduation placements of the 92-93 school year (beginning of behavioral intervention) show that students placed into classes for children with autism dropped over 22%, down to 45%. Students placed into MIS community classes for children with mild delays rose 16% to 49%, and we see the first students placed into neighborhood kindergarten classes (a total of 5%).

Graduation placements from 93-94 through 95-96 show similar

results. Placements of students into special education classes for the autistic continue to decrease, reaching a low of 29% in 94-95. Placements of students into neighborhood kindergarten classes continued to rise, hitting a high of 15% in 94-95. Students being placed into neighborhood classes for students with mild delays stayed relatively consistent, ranging from 56-59%. In all years, graduation placement decisions were made by the New York City Committee on Special Education. Their criteria for student placement did not change during the years under consideration.

For statistical purposes, the years under consideration were broken down into sets of two years. The first two years represent the pre-behavioral years. The next two years represent the beginning of the program and the changeover to the behavioral model. The third set of two years represent the final two years of analysis, after the procedures were firmly established in the preschool.

Statistical analysis of the data indicated an overall significant difference (Chi-square, M-L p = .038) between the years under analysis. Additionally, there was a significant difference between the rates of students placed into classes for the autistic versus the MIS classes between years one and two versus years three and four (Chi-square, M-L p = .049). As regards placement of students into kindergarten, there was a significant difference between the first two years of analysis and the final two years of analysis (Chi-square, M-L, p = .034).

Analysis of follow-up data indicated that three of the students placed into the MIS classes returned to the agency for school-age placement. They were unable to be maintained within their school-age placements due to behavior management issues. These students, however, were all placed into classes within the school age program of the agency that were structured with a staffing level and curriculum similar to the MIS classes. All were able to leave the school for Less Restrictive Placements within two years.

Discussion

The current data demonstrate that a change in philosophy and methodology led to marked increases in students being placed into Less Restrictive Environments. The success of the students in their placements, with only three returning, strongly suggest that their placements were indeed appropriate and not motivated by factors other than student ability.

Agencies such as AMAC have been charged with the task of placing preschool students into less restrictive environments. The current data demonstrate that attending preschool in and of itself does not necessarily result in student improvement. What the current data also demonstrate is that a properly designed special education environment can achieve the end of helping students to reach their maximum potential and reach the Least Restrictive Environment. We believe that components that are crucial to this success are:

1.   A commitment to demonstrably effective methods of instruction that emphasize changing staff behavior in keeping with behavioral analyses,

2.   On-going staff training across disciplines to ensure that interventions are carried out consistently across disciplines,

3.   Increasing density of reinforcement of appropriate student and staff behavior,

4.   Changing the focus of intervention to person-centered planning rather than intrapsychic milieu deficiencies,

5.   Related services becoming a "push in" rather than "pull out" model,

6.   Retraining of all staff in concepts of functional analysis and data collection,

7.   The institution of an agency-wide token economy to manage inappropriate behavior and encourage appropriate behavior,

8.   Creating individualized behavior treatment plans for managing student behavior, and monitoring the effectiveness of programs and interventions,

9.   The elimination of techniques that were not supported in the empirical literature,

10.   Individualizing lesson plans and the institution of a curriculum based upon the skills students would need to succeed in less restrictive environments, rather than some theoretical developmental sequence.

This structure was specifically created for students with autistic spectrum disorders, in view of their particular difficulties in learning. These difficulties may be due to an inability to perceive relevant aspects of the environment. If students are unable to differentiate relevant from irrelevant aspects of the environment, they will struggle to be able to learn in a group-oriented situation. They will similarly be frustrated in attempts to imitate peer behavior or benefit from peer models. The brain of the preschooler with autism requires a different curriculum to support proper development (Cohen, 1994). It is a mismatch of student to curriculum to attempt to teach via normalized curriculum models.

The mandate that the majority of special education preschool students should be served in a less restrictive environment is a worthy one. We have shown how students can be prepared to enter mainstream community placements. By delivering intensive, early, and effective instruction, students learn the skills that allow them to enter less restrictive environments in the mainstream continuum armed with the tools that allow them to succeed. As a final note, it is relevant that the staffing ratio of seven students to two instructors did not allow for intensive Discrete Trial Teaching, as has become synonymous with behavioral instruction in the popular image of behavior analysis of late. While increased staffing and the institution of Discrete Trial Teaching would no doubt have increased the program's effectiveness, the current data suggest that dramatic improvements can be made even in the absence of such instruction.

Appendixes:
Some Summary Presentations

(Note: these presentations were made at various times and may include some repetition. So sue me, the points bear repeating).

Presentation One:
What ABA is and is NOT
- Bobby Newman, Ph.D., B.C.B.A.
- The Dark Overlord of ABA

Applied Behavior Analysis (ABA)
- The application of the science of behavior to socially significant human behavior.

The word is behavior, not behaviorAL
- Dammit, I hate that!

ABA is not Discrete Trial Teaching!!!!!!!!
- Not even a little bit.
- Make this mistake under penalty of death by torture.
- DTT is only one of ABA's thousands of techniques.

Philosophy of ABA
- DETERMINISM: all behavior is governed by the laws of behavior and therefore there is a reason for all behavior.
- We can PREDICT AND CONTROL behavior when we discover the variables governing a particular behavior.

Data-based Decision Making

• Techniques in ABA, including when to implement and change techniques, are based upon objective (behavioral changes observable by an outside agent) criteria.

Dead Man's (Person's) Test

• Anything a dead person can do is not behavior
• Stopping someone from doing something is not a treatment plan. You must work on what they should do INSTEAD.

Single-Subject Designs

• Individual analyses are conducted, not relying on group results or averages.

Socially Significant

• The emphasis is on socially significant behavior, not statistically significant behavior.
• If your behavioral improvement does not measurably improve the student's life, you have more work to do.

Emphasis on reinforcers, not punishers

• Using aversives leads to side-effects not seen with the use of reinforcers (avoidance, counter-aggression, loss of reinforcer value, negative reinforcement of punishing behavior on the part of the teacher, etc.).

Observable behavior is the subject matter

- We measure behavior that we can see and while we do discuss internal states, they are inferred from behavior and not directly measured.

Emphasis on Here and Now

- The search is for variables maintaining behavior now, not what caused the behavior in the first place.

Criteria for behavior goals are stated very exactly

- What must he do?
- How much of it?
- Under what circumstances?

All behavioral techniques are done above-board

- There is no manipulation. All techniques are observable and knowable by the public.

Internal states frowned on as explanations (e.g., "he's lazy")

- We look for the variables maintaining behavior.

Presentation Two:
Setting up an ABA program
- Bobby Newman, Ph.D., B.C.B.A.
- The Dark Overlord of ABA

Applied Behavior Analysis (ABA)
- The application of the science of behavior to socially significant human behavior.

First Things First
- Decide if this is what you want to do.
- ABA is not a related service, it is a 24 hour a day philosophy and set of techniques. Doing it halfway can be quite destructive (e.g., you may intermittently reinforce inappropriate behavior).

Attempting to combine philosophies may not work
- "Oh, you want to be a pizza!" (when a student is aggressive, do we put that on extinction as ABA MIGHT suggest, or do we provide a sensory experience such as Sensory Integration might suggest?).

What do you need? (part one)
- Someone who knows ABA, not just some discrete trial teaching programs (hopefully a B.C.B.A. or equivalent) to coach.
- Several people to be trained to provide treatment (let's say four, but that varies).

• A family that will carry through ALL THE REST OF THE TIME.

What do you need? (part two)
• Schedule a given number of hours a week to provide intensive practice.
• Schedule time to work on generalization, or realize that you're just doing it as a default response the rest of the day.
• Schedule family members to do at least one full session a week.

What will it generally entail?
• Intensive teaching (POSSIBLY discrete trial) in various skills, everything from self-help to academic to language to social to play.
• Behavior Management procedures to reduce any behavior that is competing with the learning process.

Get Organized
• A binder should be set up and divided into sections for current programs, graphs, progress notes, maintenance, assessments, etc.
• Collect materials you will need for teaching into bins that will be available at a moment's notice.
• Copy a zillion data forms.

BEGIN ASSESSMENTS
• Baseline skills (language, cognitive, self-help, social, play, imitation, etc.).
• Do reinforcer assessments, update these at least monthly.

- Have a wide variety of reinforcers of different types (primary, social, activity, etc.). Make these as normalizing AS POSSIBLE. Use primaries if you need 'em.

Hold on, this could get a little weird!
- Avoidance behavior on the part of the student is common in the early stages, be aware of the dreaded "extinction burst." This varies tremendously from student to student. Most experienced people carry physical scars.
- Progress is rarely uniform. A student may seem to "have" a skill one day and not produce it the next day.

Think of progress in terms of performance, not learning
- Progress is generally incremental. Is that a gradual learning of a concept like "red," or a gradual acquisition of the ABILITY TO IDENTIFY it?
- I'd argue for the latter. We're retraining a brain to produce responses on request (the theory I subscribe to).

Think globally, act locally
- Begin where the student is.
- Always have in mind that we need to EVENTUALLY work AWAY from such structured teaching, helping the student to learn to learn in group settings with less formalized procedures.
- A program might start with 1 to 1 trials and end by "shadowing" in school.

Philosophy of ABA
- DETERMINISM: all behavior is governed by the laws of behavior and therefore there is a reason for all behavior.
- We can PREDICT AND CONTROL behavior when we discover the variables governing a particular behavior.

Data-based Decision Making
- Techniques in ABA, including when to implement and change techniques, are based upon objective (behavioral changes observable by an outside agent) criteria.

Dead Man's (Person's) Test
- Anything a dead person can do is not behavior.
- Stopping someone from doing something is not a treatment plan. You must work on what they should do INSTEAD.

Single-Subject Designs
- Individual analyses are conducted, not relying on group results or averages.

Socially Significant
- The emphasis is on socially significant behavior, not statistically significant behavior.
- If your behavioral improvement does not measurably improve the student's life, you have more work to do.

Emphasis on reinforcers, not punishers

• Using aversives leads to side-effects not seen with the use of reinforcers (avoidance, counter-aggression, loss of reinforcer value, negative reinforcement of punishing behavior on the part of the teacher, etc.).

Observable behavior is the subject matter

• We measure behavior that we can see and while we do discuss internal states, they are inferred from behavior and not directly measured.

Emphasis on Here and Now

• The search is for variables maintaining behavior now, not what caused the behavior in the first place.

Criteria for behavior goals are stated very exactly

• What must he do?
• How much of it?
• Under what circumstances?

All behavioral techniques are done above-board

• There is no manipulation. All techniques are observable and knowable by the public.

Internal states frowned on as explanations (e.g., "he's lazy")

- We look for the variables maintaining behavior.

Presentation Three:
Functional Analysis of Behavior

- Bobby Newman, Ph.D., B.C.B.A.
- The Dark Overlord of ABA

THE CENTRAL QUESTION

- Why is he DOING that?
- (not why did he start)
- What are the variables maintaining behavior now?

Step 1

- Define the behavior in such a way that everyone can agree when it has happened and when it has not.

Step 2

- Come up with an appropriate measurement system (e.g., frequency, rate, percentage, latency, magnitude, duration, etc.).

Step 3

- BASELINE!!!!!!!
- Observe the behavior to get a level for comparison purposes and collect A--> B --> C   Data.
- (Antecedent --> Behavior --> Consequence)

Step 4

- Draft a hypothesis regarding the variables controlling behavior based upon what is observed during baseline.

Step 5
• Test your hypothesis by carrying out the treatment plan logically suggested by your hypothesis. If it does not work, reassess. Did you carry out the plan improperly, or is it the wrong plan? Back to step three.

Effective Behavior Management Requires TWO things:
• First you must pick the correct variables maintaining behavior.
• You must then carry out the treatment plan properly and consistently.

INCONSISTENCY IS OFTEN WORSE THAN DOING NOTHING!!!!!!

Presentation Four:
Back to Basics: Shaping and Chaining of Behavior

- Bobby Newman, Ph.D., B.C.B.A.
- The Dark Overlord of ABA

Shaping
- The creation of new behavior by reinforcing approximations to a desired behavior.

Chaining
- Combining several smaller behaviors to make one long, complex behavior.

Forward Chaining
- This can be done via forward chaining (teach first step first, second step second and so on until one completely teaches the behavior), or

Backward Chaining
- This can be done via backward chaining (prompt the student through the full behavior, working on the last step in the chain first, and, when this is mastered, working on teaching the last step AND the next to last step, etc., until one completely teaches the behavior).

To Shape a Behavior, Part One
- Find the best approximation to the desired ("target") behavior.
- Reinforce that approximation.

- When behavior is reliable, place the approximation on extinction (i.e., DO NOT REINFORCE IT).
- An extinction burst will set in, and this will increase behavioral variability.
- Seek a variation that is closer to the desired or target behavior.
- Reinforce that closer approximation.
- Go back to step #2, reinforce the new, better approximation.
- Continue until the behavior is perfect.

To Shape a Behavior, Final Considerations

- Go to an intermittent reinforcement schedule on the perfect behavior.
- Work towards generalization and maintenance.

To chain a behavior

- Create a task analysis of the behavior to be taught.
- A task analysis is a written description of all the steps a person must perform in order to complete a behavior.
- HINT FOR WRITING TASK ANALYSES: perform the behavior yourself, talking out loud into a tape recorder, describing each step as you perform it.

A pre-written task analysis is JUST A STARTING POINT!

- Task analyses must be constantly re-written based upon student progress.
- If a student is having difficulty with a given step, break the step down further.
- A task analysis that begins as seven steps may end up being 107 steps.

Presentation Five:
Introduction to Discrete Trial Teaching
- Bobby Newman, Ph.D., B.C.B.A.
- The Dark Overlord of ABA

Discrete Trial Teaching
- The application of the A --> B --> C three term contingency to the teaching situation.
- It is theoretically necessary because of the difficulties many people with disabilities have in learning information from the generalized environment.

ABA is not Discrete Trial Teaching!!!!!!!!
- Not even a little bit.
- Make this mistake under penalty of death by the torture of having to listen to Top 40 CD's.
- DTT is only one of ABA's thousands of techniques.

DTT moves in units, quantum mechanics versus Newtonian
- Each "trial" is a separate attempt to teach or reinforce a previously learned behavior.
- It is not a free-flowing discussion, it is distinct packets (antecedent instruction and then behavior and then consequence, A --> B --> C).

Go for what is functional first

• What's the point of knowing that the opposite of live is dead or being able to know who the prime minister is if you can't play independently for five minutes, make an initiation to a peer, or toilet yourself?

Varying Terminology

• Different programs may refer to the same concept by different names (e.g., "mastered" versus "maintenance," "randomized" versus "expanded trial").

• Translate whatever terms you use into the three term contingency.

Antecedent

• The thing the teacher does to signal the behavior.
• Also called the instruction.
• Also called the S^D (Ess Dee).
• Varies from program to program.

Behavior

• What the student does in response to the instruction.
• Also called the Response.
• What is required may vary from program to program and person to person (e.g., shaping responses and where one is in the progression of programs).

Consequence

- In DTT, the consequence is almost always a positive reinforcer.
- A positive reinforcer is a consequence that INCREASES the probability of a future behavior when PRESENTED following a behavior.
- Reinforcers are highly individualized.

Prompting Strategies

- There are several types of prompting strategies (e.g., errorless learning and no-no prompting).
- What technique is being used may vary depending on stage of program (e.g., acquisition versus maintenance) or other considerations.
- ABA is a data-based discipline. If one strategy is not working, move to another.

Data Collection

- Data should be collected during each program delivery to assess progress.
- Different types of data might be collected, depending on program and what is appropriate (e.g., percent correct, rate or "fluency," latency to correct response, etc.).

Isolation versus Randomized Material

- When you first begin, new steps are often isolated (you work on them on their own).
- Some people want to isolate TWO steps at a time to avoid "over-learning" of one step.

- As the student masters the skill, move it into randomization (mix it up so that you work on several stops simultaneously).
- Move into maintenance once all steps are mastered in randomization.

Varying Strategies
- Different clinicians have different ideas about how to progress (e.g., in a receptive task they may or may not leave out distractors at first, they might work on more functional behavior during motor imitation as opposed to arbitrary movements).
- These differences are sometimes cosmetic, sometimes meaningful. Adjust according to student need.

Mastery Criterion
- Mastery criterion should specify skill level and conditions (e.g., 90% accurate or above, across three sessions and two teachers, with 2 distractors present, as one example).

Assume Nothing!
- Baseline all skills. Check what the student can do and program accordingly in terms of what the student needs to learn to be able to make it in less restrictive settings.
- Some behaviors are actually multiple concepts (e.g., "yes" and "no" for factual info versus preferences, etc.).

Receptive versus Expressive

- Acting on instructions (e.g., RECEPTIVELY touching a ball) is a totally different skill than EXPRESSIVELY identifying an indicated object by verbally naming it).
- You may need to work on both. Don't assume that because a student can do one that he can do another.
- Don't do this one after the other, mix it up (otherwise you provide an unfair cue).

Go for Generalization

- Generalization does not spontaneously occur without programming for it.
- Failure to generalize is one of the hallmarks of the autistic-spectrum disorders.

Move to loose teaching as soon as possible

- As the student masters the skill, move to loose teaching.
- Vary the cues, where you do the practice, the people doing the practice, the phrasing of questions, the time of day, the order of programs, the clothing worn, etc.
- It is the Dr. Seuss approach: do it in a house and do it with a mouse, do it on a train and do it on a plane, do it with a fox and in a box……….

Not on handout, what programs?

• This is not on a handout because it varies tremendously and cookie cutters are the bane of well-designed programs....

However, as a GENERAL idea....

• Begin by ASSESSING the following:
• Attending skills (e.g., eye to face contact)
• Motor imitation
• Verbal imitation
• Labels
• Requests
• Matching
• Object Identification
• Using yes/no functionally
• Self-help skills (toileting, dressing, etc.)
• Social initiations
• Independent play
• Social play

Presentation Six: Random Tips on Behavior Management

- Bobby Newman, Ph.D., B.C.B.A.
- The Dark Overlord of ABA

Never make a promise you can't keep

- If you say that things will be a particular way, they must be that way.
- Instructional control only establishes when you specify what a contingency will be and then it happens as you said it would.

Do not repeat yourself!

- Repeating yourself merely teaches the person that it is fine to ignore you, you'll just repeat the cue.
- Give ONE verbal cue, and follow with a physical prompt if necessary.

Always program for generalization

- While using the same verbal cue all the time (for example) may lead to greater success initially, you are making a "deal with the devil" in that you will have to use that same cue forever to ensure compliance.

REINFORCE behavior that you want to see

- Do not assume that a person should do a behavior for its own sake.

- Students will "go on strike" if reinforcement is not forthcoming or of sufficient quality or quantity.

"Catch 'em being good!"
- That's it.

Treatment plans must be based upon the function of the behavior
- There is no such thing as a generic plan, you must design individual plans for individual behavior by individual people.
- Make sure treatment plans make sense (e.g., do not use time out for avoidance behavior).
- You can do the wrong plan until pop singers stop being annoying. It will STILL be counter-productive or useless.

Strive towards normalized reinforcers
- Chances for maintenance will be maximized when naturally occurring reinforcers can come to control the behavior.

Remember the effects of intermittent reinforcement
- Continuous reinforcement leads to behavior that has little resistance to extinction and leads to a large extinction burst when reinforcement stops.
- Intermittent reinforcement leads to behavior that has a great deal of resistance to extinction.

Presentation Seven:
To Promote Generalization
- Dana R. Reinecke, MA, BCABA
- The Dark Mommy of ABA

Types of generalization:
A. Stimulus generalization/transfer of training - generality across stimuli, people, and conditions.
B. Response generalization/concomitant behavior change - development of related behaviors not specifically trained.

Maintenance/resistance to extinction:
- behavior changes that persist over time.

Strategies for promoting maintenance:
A. Aim for natural contingencies of reinforcement; try to train the most relevant responses that will be most maintained by the environment.
B. Use intermittent and delayed reinforcement to prevent discrimination of situations when responses will be reinforced.
C. Use self-management techniques.

Strategies for promoting generalization:

A. Train sufficient examples of the response.
B. Program common stimuli.
C. Train loosely:
- use more than one teacher
- teach in more than one place
- teach in a variety of positions
- vary tone of voice
- vary choice of words
- show stimuli from a variety of angles
- vary reinforcers
- vary times of day
- reinforce variability in responding.
- reinforce responding to variable stimuli.

How parents can help professionals:

A. Know the program.
B. Help choose the skills to be addressed.
C. Ask how to carry through.
D. Speak up if being asked to do something impossible or impractical.
E. Take data.
F. Keep assessing reinforcers.
G. Teach at every possible opportunity and create teaching opportunities throughout the day.
H. Commit completely. Don't trust blindly, but give things a chance to work.

Presentation Eight:
ABA is supposed to BUILD autonomy
- Bobby Newman, Ph.D., B.C.B.A.
- The Dark Overlord of ABA

Sun Tzu, THE ART OF WAR
- If you know yourself, but do not know the enemy, you will win 50 of 100 battles.
- If you know your enemy, but do not know yourself, you will win 50 of 100 battles.
- If you know the enemy and know yourself, you need not fear the result of 100 battles.

They just don't like us:
Kohlberg (1983, p. X)
- "Though valid for explaining many research findings, Skinner's theory is not a valid educational theory in the sense of being a basis for good educational practice, a good theory for teachers to learn and follow. Skinner may dispense with ideas of freedom and dignity to arrive at a theory valid for explaining studies of reward in animals and children. A theory 'beyond freedom and dignity' must, however, have serious flaws as a guide to teacher behavior. A theory that ignores freedom and dignity in the learning process leads to the practice of constructing 'teacher proof' materials. It also leads to kits designed to be 'student proof,' that is, to modify the student's behavior without his understanding or assent to the theory and methods applied to him."

Sir Karl Popper

• refused to sign THE HUMANIST MANIFESTO TWO because Skinner, "an enemy of freedom and democracy" had already signed. (see FREE INQUIRY 1(2), pp. 3-4 for Anthony Flew and Sidney Hook's additional objections to Skinner's involvement)

The Reluctant Alliance

• In a review of my book in the HUMANISTIC PSYCHOLOGIST, the reviewer lamented that I had equated humanism with the thinking of the American Humanist Association, of which "even B.F. Skinner was a member." (Bobby note: Skinner was AHA's Humanist of the Year in 1971).

The Clockwork Testament: Anthony Burgess

• "Well I think its bloody monsters (?). Human beings are defined by freedom of choice. Once you have them doing what theyre told is good just because theyre going to get a lump of sugar instead of a kick up the ahss (?!), then ethnics no longer exists" (p. 101, punctuation and spelling from original).

Aggeler, 1979

• "....given Skinner's apparent inability to think of man as anything but an abstract concept." (p. 96, commenting on the irony of Anthony Burgess naming the fictionalized B.F. Skinner "Man" in THE CLOCKWORK TESTAMENT)

Burgess' A Clockwork Orange, Petix, 1987

- "The white-jacketed doctors are evil, and as extreme versions of B.F. Skinner's behaviorists...understandably so" (p. 94)

Aggeler, 1979

- "Psychologists have forced upon him (Alex) what Professor Skinner might call 'the inclination to behave'...If one were seeking an illustration to place above a Skinnerian caption, such as 'the inclination to behave' or 'operant conditioning' or 'Beyond Freedom and Dignity,' one could hardly find one more vivid and arresting then...Alex licking the sole of the actor/antagonist's shoe" (pp. 174-175)

Burgess, 1978

- From his book entitled 1985: "The techniques for total manipulation of the human soul were in existence in 1932...Ivan Pavlov had four more years to live, he had done his work, and had been able to see something of the possibilities of its social application. 'How like a dog is man,' as Shakespeare, if he had read B.F. Skinner, might have said. . . .Skinner's title appalls in itself. Beyond truth, beyond beauty, beyond goodness, beyond God, beyond life. Big Brother does not go so far....What God has joined together, even though it be an unholy trinity of a human brain, let no man put asunder. Pray for Dr. Skinner. Let Pavlov rest in peace. Amen."

Walden Two commentary: Matson, 1971

• "The key to the kingdom of WALDEN TWO was operant conditioning; by this magical technique, applied to all residents from birth, the 'Hamlet syndrome' (the anxiety of choice) was effectively removed. Like that wonderful Mrs. Prothro in Dylan Thomas' Christmas story, who 'said the right thing always,' so the creatures of Skinner's novel were conditioned to make the right choices automatically. It was instant certitude, at the price of all volition. Like Pavlov's dogs, Skinner's people made only conditioned responses to the stimulus of their master's voice."

Negley and Patrick, 1952

• referred to the children of WALDEN TWO as "little guinea pigs" and spoke of the novel's "nauseating conclusion."

Frye, 1965

• "...its philistine vulgarity makes it a caricature of the pedantry of social science . . . . and shows the infantilism of specialists who see society merely as an extension of their own specialty" (p. 32)

Matson, 1976

• "There is so much that is wrong with this behavioral panacea-so much that is patently silly and morally irresponsible..." (p. 110)

Mumford, 1965

- "The sugared concept of scientific control, which B. F. Skinner insinuates into his WALDEN TWO, is another name for arrested development" (p. 10).

The Detached Intellectual: Kumar, 1987

- "It is here that the general humanist critique is most uneasily and most insecurely on the defensive. It seems concerned to preserve a 'sacred' area of human life and consciousness from the scrutiny of science. Certain cherished human values- free will, spontaneity, creativity- seem threatened by this scientific approach to human behavior.   There appears to be an anxiety that perhaps man will after all turn out not to have the god-like attributes postulated of him" (p. 369).

Now it's Our Turn:
MacCorquodale, 1971

- "...quite the contrary. Once the variables that affect behavior are firmly identified in scientific laws, man is free to alter his fate...by manipulating the variables that are already affecting his behavior for better or worse..." (p. 12)
- "Behaviorism is not really a bleak conspiracy to delimit man's choices and freedom by artificial constraint, any more than physics is a conspiracy against atoms" (p. 12)
- C'mon, you've gotta love that line.

MacCorquodale, 1971
- "Behaviorism, by locating the means of self-control outside of behavior, where they are accessible and manageable, gives man this choice" (p. 13).

Skinner, 1974
- "In the behavioristic view, man can now control his own destiny because he knows what must be done and how to do it" (p. 277)

Skinner, 1971
- "The behaviorists I know...are gentle people, deeply concerned with the problems facing us in the world today, who see a chance to bring the methods of science to bear on these problems...behaviorism IS humanism. It has the distinction of being effective humanism" (p. 35).

Key Point
- ABA does not somehow remove autonomy. A person who has not learned a behavior (or set of behaviors) DOES NOT HAVE CHOICE. The person can NOT engage in the behavior under consideration. They just don't "know how."

I CAN wash dishes
- I simply pretend I can't.
- Those who CAN have a choice: do it or don't do it (based upon determining variables).

I   CAN   occupy   my   time   with constructive behavior.

- I simply choose not to
- Tivo is taping Xena and Get Smart for me as you read this.

Self-management training

- Self-management training is the ultimate step in ABA, providing autonomy to the individual in that (s)he can now encourage and discourage behavior in the absence of an outside agent (and revisit MacCorquodale quote regarding manipulation of one's own destiny).

Parent Quote to Bobby, Durham, England, 2001

- "When we formed this group, we agreed that we wouldn't push each other and try to get the other parents to do the same type of treatment we were doing. My husband and I thought "Growing Minds" was the way to go, and we silently plotted to break the rules and convince the other parents to abandon ABA. It just seemed so against everything we believed in. Then we heard you speak and saw you working with the kids. Had we seen that first, we would have gone with ABA."

A touching moment

- Bobby to parent: "that's the nicest thing anyone has ever said to me."

References and Suggested Reading

Aggeler, G. (1979). *Anthony Burgess: The artist as novelist.* University, Alabama: University of Alabama Press.

Ayllon, T. & Azrin, N. H. (1964). Reinforcement and instructions with mental patients. *Journal of the Experimental Analysis of Behavior, 7,* 327-331.

Bailey, J. S. (1991). Promoting freedom and dignity: A new agenda for behavior analysis. Paper presented at the annual convention of the Association for Behavior Analysis, May 1991.

Bijou, S. W. (1970). What psychology has to offer education- now. *Journal of Applied Behavior Analysis, 3,* 65-71.

Binder, C., & Watkins, C.L. (1989). Promoting effective instructional methods: Solutions to America's educational crisis. *Future Choices, 1*(3), 33-39.

Burgess, A. (1978). *1985.* Boston, MA: Little, Brown and Company.

Burgess, A. (1974). *The clockwork testament.* New York: Alfred A. Knopf Publishing.

Camarta, S. M. & Nelson, K. E. (1992). Treatment efficiency as a function of target selection in the remediation of child language disorders. *Clinical Linguistics and Phonetics, 6,* 167-178.

Carr, E. G., & Durand, V. M. (1985). Reducing behavior problems through functional communication training. *Journal of Applied Behavior Analysis, 18,* 111-126.

Chumpelik, D. (1984). The PROMPT system of therapy: Theoretical framework and applications for developmental apraxia of speech. *Seminars in Speech and Language, 5,* 139-156.

Cohen, I. L. (1994). Artificial neural network analogues of learning in autism. *Biological Psychiatry, 36,* 5-20.

Cooper, J.O., Heron, T.E., & Heward, W.L. (1987). *Applied behavior analysis.* Toronto: Merrill Publishing.

Foxx, R. M. (1982). *Increasing behavior of persons with severe retardation and autism.* Champaign, IL: Research Press.

Freed, D. B., Marshall, R. C., & Frazier, K. E. (1997). Long-term effectiveness of PROMPT treatment in a severely apractic-aphasic speaker. *Aphasiology, 11,* 342-365.

Frye, N. (1965). Varieties of literary utopias. In F.E. Manuel (Ed.), *Utopias and utopian thought* (pp. 25-49). Boston, MA: Houghton Mifflin.

Goetz, E.M. & Baer, D. M. (1974). Social control of form diversity and the emergence of new forms in children's blockbuilding. *Journal of Applied Behavior Analysis, 6,* 209-217.

Green, G. (1996). Evaluating claims about treatments for autism. In Maurice, C., Green, G., & Luce, S. C. (Eds.). *Behavioral interventions for young children with autism* (pp. 15-28). Austin, TX: Pro-Ed.

Guralick, M.J. (1998). Effectiveness of early intervention for vulnerable children: A developmental perspective. *American Journal of Mental Retardation, 102,* 319-345.

Koegel, R. L., & Koegel, L. K. (1995). *Teaching children with autism: Strategies for initiating positive interactions and improving learning opportunities.* Baltimore: Paul H. Brookes.

Koegel, R. L., O'Dell, M., & Dunlap, G. (1988). Producing speech use in nonverbal autistic children by reinforcing attempts. *Journal of Autism and Developmental Disorders, 18,* 525-538.

Kohlberg, L. (1983). Foreword. In J. Reimer, D. P. Paolitto, R. H. Hersh *Promoting moral growth.*   New York: Longman.

Kumar, K. (1987). *Utopia and anti-utopia in modern times.* New York: Basil Blackwell.

Lovaas, O. I. (1987). Behavioral treatment and normal educational and intellectual functioning in young autistic children. *Journal of Consulting and Clinical Psychology, 55,* 3-9.

Lovaas, O. I. (1981). *Teaching developmentally disabled children: The ME book.* Austin: Pro-Ed.

Malott, R. W. (1989). The achievement of evasive goals: Control by rules describing contingencies that are not direct acting. In S.C. Hayes (Ed.) *Rule-governed behavior: Cognition, contingencies and instructional control* (pp. 269-322). New York: Plenum Press.

MacCorquodale, K. (1971). Behaviorism is a humanism. *The Humanist, 31*(2), 11-12.

Matson, F. W. (1976). *The idea of man.* New York: Delacorte Press.

Matson, F.W. (1971). Humanistic theory: The third revolution in psychology. *The Humanist, 31*(2), 7-11.

Maurice, C., Green, G., & Luce, S. C. (1996) *Behavioral Intervention for Young Children with Autism.* Austin: Pro-Ed.

Needelman, M. (2000). My role as a related service provider at an ABA school for children with autism. In Newman, Reinecke, & Newman (Eds.) *Words from those who care: Further case studies of ABA with people with autism* (pp. 130-138). New York: Dove and Orca.

Negley, G., & Patrick, J. M. (1952). *The quest for utopia: An anthology of imaginary societies.* New York: Henry Schuman.

New York State Department of Health Early Intervention Program (1999). *Clinical Practice Guideline: Report of the Recommendations, Autism and Pervasive Developmental Disorders,* New York State Department of Health Early Intervention Program.

Newman, B. (in press). Extraordinary claims require extraordinary proof: On including new technology into ABA programs and responding to questions regarding different programs. *Science in Autism Treatments.*

Newman, B. (1999). *When everybody cares: Case studies of ABA with people with autism.* New York: Dove and Orca.

Newman, B. (1992). *The reluctant alliance: Behaviorism and humanism.* Buffalo, NY: Prometheus Books.

Newman, B., Buffington, D. M., & Hemmes, N. S. (1996). External and self-reinforcement used to increase the appropriate conversation of autistic teenagers. *Education and Training in Mental Retardation and Developmental Disabilities, 31,* 304-309.

Newman, B., Buffington, D.M., Hemmes, N.S., & Rosen, D. (1997). Answering objections to self-management and related concepts. *Behavior and Social Issues, 6*(2), 85-95.

Newman, B., Buffington, D.M., O'Grady, M.A., McDonald, M.E., Poulson, C.L., & Hemmes, N.S. (1995). Self-management of schedule-following in three teenagers with autism. *Behavioral Disorders, 20*(3), 195-201.

Newman, B., Lyttle, R., & Bohonos, A. (2000). Incidental versus discrete trial teaching compared for skill acquisition and competing behavior for children with autism. Presented at the annual convention of the Association for Behavior Analysis, Washington, D.C.

Newman, B. & Needelman, M. (2000). On the role of related service providers in an ABA-based school. Presented at the annual conference of the New York State Association for Behavior Analysis, Saratoga.

Newman, B., Needelman, M., Reinecke, D. R., Robek, A. (In press). The effect of providing choices on skill acquisition and competing behavior of children with autism during discrete trial instruction. *Behavioral Interventions.*

Newman, B., Reinecke, D. R., & Meinberg, D. (2000). Self-management of varied responding in children with autism. *Behavioral Interventions, 15,* 145-151.

Newman, B., Reinecke, D. R., & Newman, L. (2000). *Words from those who care: Further case studies of ABA with people with autism.* New York: Dove and Orca.

Newman, B., Tuntigian, L, Ryan, C. S., & Reinecke, D. R. (1997). Self-management of a DRO procedure by three students with autism. *Behavioral Interventions, 12,* 149-156.

Petix, E. (1987). Linguistics, mechanics, and metaphysics: A Clockwork Orange. In H. Bloom (Ed.) *Modern Critical Views: Anthony Burgess* (pp. 85-96). New York: Chelsea House.

Rappaport, M. F. (2001). Notes from the speech pathologist's office. In Maurice, C., Green, G., & Foxx, R. M. (Eds.). *Making a difference: Behavior interventions for autism* (pp. 163-180). Austin, TX: Pro-Ed.

Reinecke, D. R., Newman, B., & Meinberg, D. (1999). Self-management of sharing in preschoolers with autism. *Education and Training in Mental Retardation, 34,* 312-317.

Sidman, M. (1989). *Coercion and its fallout.* Boston: Authors Cooperative

Skinner, B. F. (1976). The ethics of helping people. *The Humanist, 36*(1), 7-11.

Skinner, B. F. (1974). *About behaviorism.* New York: Random House.

Skinner, B. F. (1972). Humanism and behaviorism. *The Humanist, 32*(4), 18-20.

Skinner, B. F. (1971). Humanistic behaviorism. *The Humanist, 31*(3), 35.

Skinner, B. F. (1953). *Science and human behavior.* New York: The Free Press.

Square, P. A., Cumpelik, D. A., Morningstar, D., & Adams, S. (1986). Efficacy of the prompt system of therapy for treatment of acquired aphasia of speech: A follow-up investigation. *Clinical Aphasiology Conference Proceedings.* Minnesota: Bek Publishers.

Sundberg, M. L., & Partington, J. W. (1998). *Teaching language to children with autism or other developmental disabilities.* Pleasant Hill, CA: Behavior Analysts, Inc.

Van Houten, R., Axelrod, S., Bailey, J. S., Favell, J. E., Foxx, R. M., Iwata, B. A., & Lovaas, O. I. (1988). The right to effective behavioral treatment. *Journal of Applied Behavior Analysis, 21,* 381-384.

Yoder, P. J., Kaiser, A. P., Alpert, C., & Fischer, R. (1993). Following the child's lead when teaching nouns to preschoolers with mental retardation. *Journal of Speech and Hearing Research, 36,* 158-167.

About the Authors

<u>Sarah Birch, M.S.ed</u> Sarah Birch has worked with both children and adults diagnosed with autistic-spectrum disorders since 1993. Sarah has served as a direct care worker, vocational trainer, classroom teacher, master teacher, program director, and currently works as an ABA supervisor for an early intervention program. In addition to working directly with individuals and families, Sarah has worked on a variety of research projects. Her work has been published in several professional journals. She has presented with her colleagues at the annual ABA and NYSABA conferences. Sarah is currently working towards her doctorate and completing the requirements for the B.C.B.A.

<u>Frederica Blausten, M.A., M.S.</u> Frederica Blausten is recognized as a specialist and motivational leader in the Human Services area. She is an experienced executive in all phases of agency operation. In the ten years under her direction, AMAC has grown from 40 to 350 families and has gained positive professional and national recognition. AMAC's growth has been multi-facted, including improved, more secure facilities, enhanced educational programs, expanded family training and support, increased governmental funding, and the development of staff. Ms. Blausten's leadership and professionalism directly impacts on all aspects of the agency and creates an environment focused on individual care for all AMAC's students. Many of AMAC's programs have served as a model for agencies servicing autistic children throughout New York State and California.

<u>Bobby Newman, Ph.D., B.C.B.A.</u> Bobby is a New York State licensed psychologist and Board Certified Behavior Analyst. He is the author of several books and articles on the history and philosophy of ABA, the treatment of autism, and behavior therapy for other clinical syndromes. Bobby hosted WEVD-AM's live radio call-in show dealing with issues in developmental disabilities, <u>When Everybody Cares</u>. Bobby is the Past-President for the New York State Association for Behavior Analysis. Affectionately known as the Dark Overlord of ABA, Bobby provides staff training and direct clinical service at AMAC, for several school districts around New York State, as well as programs in England, Ireland, and Northern Ireland. For this work, Bobby has been honored by several local and international parents' groups.

<u>Dana R. Reinecke, Ph.D., B.C.B.A.</u>   Dana is a Board Certified Behavior Analyst.   She recently completed her Ph.D. in Applied Behavior Analysis at the Learning Processes program of The Graduate School and University Center, CUNY.   Dana provides consultation to school districts providing services to children diagnosed with autistic-spectrum disorders.   She has published in several behavioral and developmental disabilities journals, and has presented at national and international conferences.